# The Foreign Policy of John Rawls and Amartya Sen

# The Foreign Policy of John Rawls and Amartya Sen

## Neal Leavitt

LEXINGTON BOOKS
Lanham • Boulder • New York • London

Published by Lexington Books
A wholly owned subsidary of Rowman & Littlefield
4501 Forbes Boulevard, Suite 200, Lanham, Maryland 20706
www.rowman.com

Unit A, Whitacre Mews, 26-34 Stannary Street, London SE11 4AB

British Library Cataloguing in Publication Information Available

**Library of Congress Cataloging-in-Publication Data**

The hardback edition of this book was previously catalogued by the Library of Congress as follows:

Leavitt, Neal, 1974-
The foreign policy of John Rawls and Amartya Sen / Neal Leavitt.
pages cm
Includes bibliographical references and index.
1. Rawls, John, 1921-2002. 2. Sen, Amartya, 1933- 3. International relations--Moral and ethical
aspects. 4. International relations--Philosophy. I. Title.
JZ1306.L428 2013
327.101--dc23
2013022849

ISBN 978-0-7391-8176-8 (cloth : alk. paper)
ISBN 978-1-4985-1547-4 (pbk. : alk. paper)
ISBN 978-0-7391-8177-5 (electronic)

∞™ The paper used in this publication meets the minimum requirements of American
National Standard for Information Sciences Permanence of Paper for Printed Library
Materials, ANSI/NISO Z39.48-1992.

Printed in the United States of America

# Contents

# Acknowledgements

I would like to thank my colleagues at Boston University, Natalie McKnight, Robert Wexelblatt, Michael Kort, Adam Sweeting, Tom Whalen, Andy Andres, Paul Thur, Alan Taylor, and Alyse Bithavas-Glac for their interest and encouragement as I worked on this project. Much thanks is owed to Yonatan Grad for many and varied discussions of public health and David Reich for his enthusiasm in matters intellectual. Irene above all has helped me along.

# Preface

The interpretation I provide of John Rawls' text *The Law of Peoples* is founded on contrasting descriptions of the political relation—that is, the relationship between civilians, heads of state, and the armed forces in a society.

In Rawls' interpretation of the social contract, the civilian population of the society centers the regime. In particular, civilians elect heads of state. These elected representatives, in turn, pledge to protect the rights of the civilian population. And in this picture of political life, the armed forces of a society help heads of state achieve this goal.

The social contract tradition—as interpreted by Rawls—elevates civilians within the regime. In political realism, however, the civilian population does not center the regime. Instead, political realism focuses on the hierarchy created by the existence of an army. More precisely: in political realism the difference in power between the commander of an army and the unarmed members of society is so great as to be a difference in kind; there is no proportion between an armed person and an unarmed person in any society. As a consequence, political realism tends to describe the state almost entirely in terms of its military strength and does not focus on the concept of rights.

The two pictures of the political relation yield two very different pictures of foreign policy. The foreign policy of political realism centers on the strength of the state's armed forces: a state must be militarily stronger than its competitors to maintain itself. Rawls' foreign policy, however, focuses on promoting the basic human rights of all persons around the globe. The possibility of agreements between nations is also stressed.

In the interpretation I offer of *The Law of Peoples*, Rawls is primarily operating within the human rights tradition. That is, a main objective of *The Law of Peoples* is to advance human rights. However, Rawls does not completely break free of the perspective of political realism in this text. In particular, Rawls believes established democracies must maintain a nuclear arsenal and must be willing to use conventional weapons—and possibly nuclear weapons—against the civilian populations of outlaw regimes in situations of "supreme emergency." In this way, democracies can avoid situations of excessive military weakness relative to expansionist states.

Rawls criticizes—but does not entirely break free from—political realism: there is a strand of "defensive political realism" within his foreign policy. In order to emphasize this point, I develop Amartya Sen's criticism of nuclear deterrence as a strategy for defense. Sen, unlike Rawls, never endorses the supreme emergency exemption. Sen also focuses on the need for nuclear disarmament and the possibility of using revenues freed up by disarmament for development goals. As such, Sen offers a more definitive break with political realism—and his foreign policy is better aligned with the aim of protecting civilians.

# Introduction

The social contract is a recurring theme in John Rawls' political writings and in the culture at large: many reflections on political life invoke this idea.[1] But what, exactly, is a social contract? And why invoke the social contract to handle the problems of the day?

At the most basic level, a social contract defines the relationship between civilians, heads of state, and the armed forces of a society. In this picture of political life, civilians *agree* to follow a government in exchange for protection and security. There is a contract or compact between civilians, heads of state, and the armed forces of a society that is the basis of a regime.

Interpreted in this way, a social contract makes explicit the power relations in a society. The relation between civilians, heads of state and the armed forces is founded on an agreement. But it is not enough to claim that any type of agreement between civilians and heads of state is sufficient to create a society. The kind of agreement is also important. The agreement must be just or fair in order to be valid.

Thus, on a second level, a social contract defines the legitimacy of a regime. More precisely, in Rawls' interpretation of the social contract, a government is not legitimate unless its citizens believe it is legitimate. In a just regime, *the beliefs* of citizens are politically relevant.

On this interpretation, a social contract takes the extraordinarily complicated and shifting web of political life and distills from it a central ideal. A just society is formed through an agreement that all members of this society can accept. A just society is the outcome of the free choices of its citizenry.

Conversely, a state in which a small group of individuals is able to command the armed forces of a nation—without elections—does more than concentrate extraordinary powers in the hands of a few people.[2] It also marginalizes the beliefs of citizens to an extreme degree. The thoughts of the civilian population have no power here.

## 1. EQUALITY

Freedom of choice is central to the regime envisioned by Rawls. Citizens must consent to the rule of their government. Conversely, a regime cannot be just or fair if it is exclusively founded on the threat of force and violence. From this point of view, a just regime casts an unjust regime into relief.

The social contract establishes an ideal in which the thoughts and beliefs of individual citizens play a formative role in the behavior of government. A second ideal Rawls' associates with the social contract is the ideal of equality or equal treatment under the law.

According to the ideal of political equality, a government must treat all citizens in a similar fashion. A government must follow the same process or procedures in its dealings with citizens. In this situation, there is a consistent and predictable expression of power and control.

For example, the principles "all citizens are innocent until proven guilty" and "every citizen is entitled to a fair trial" follow the ideal of equal treatment under the law. According to these principles, a process for determining guilt or innocence—a fair trial—is unconditionally granted to all citizens.

The ideal of political equality outlines a legal process for all citizens. The ideal of political equality, however, must also be understood in terms of the actions and practices it rules out as unjust. More precisely, the ideal of political equality rules out random or unwarranted incarcerations: a government cannot arrest a citizen with impunity or make arbitrary distinctions between citizens. A government cannot deny certain groups of citizens a fair trial or due process of law.

This point can be put another way. The claim "some people are always guilty" does not satisfy the ideal of equality. Just the opposite: such a claim—if it becomes enshrined in the legal doctrines of a country and is enforced by the police or other authorities—creates a permanent underclass of subjects in a state. It allows heads of state to incarcerate and punish an individual or group of people without evidence or reason.

Similarly, the claim "some people are always innocent" does not satisfy the ideal of equality. But it fails to do so for a different reason. This claim arbitrarily elevates certain individuals within a society. Such a claim—if it becomes part of the operating procedure of a government or political authority—establishes a permanent upperclass within a state. It allows a group of people to exist beyond the reach of law and justice.

Seen in this light, the ideal of equality expands the notion of an unjust regime. A state that lacks the ideal of political equality—a state in which some individuals can be incarcerated with impunity, or a state in which some citizens can never be prosecuted for misconduct—is unjust. This state does not afford the same protections to all of its citizens.

### The Criterion of Reciprocity

So far, core aspects of a social contract have been outlined. For Rawls, a social contract is a "thought experiment" that shows how a regime can be created under the constraints of freedom and equality.[3] If every person in society asks the question "What kind of regime do I wish to live in?" a preliminary answer could be: a regime in which the freedom and equality of each citizen is acknowledged and respected.[4]

From this perspective, Rawls is part of a long line of thinkers who place freedom and equality at the forefront of political thought; Rawls' sense of freedom and equality is akin to the views of Locke, Kant and Rousseau. There are, however, features of Rawls' thought that define the social contract tradition in new ways. Also, Rawls is explicit about standards that are implicit or absent in the texts of these earlier thinkers.

Consider again the ideals of equality and freedom. In Rawls' usage, individuals consent to the rules that govern their lives in large part because these rules treat every person equally. The ideals of freedom or consent and equality work together in *The Law of Peoples*.

For example, the claim "men can own property but women cannot" clearly violates the ideal of equality. It treats men and women in different ways. It acknowledges a property right for men but denies this right to women. And if it is enacted in a state, it fosters a degree of dependency and powerlessness in women that causes substantial harm.

The claim "men can own property but women cannot" does not treat men and women in an equal manner. However, this claim is also one a woman is unlikely to consent to—if her opinion on the matter is asked. That is to say, the claim "men can own property but women cannot" does not take into account the beliefs women might have about owning property. The claim violates the ideal of consent as well as the ideal of equality.

The linkage between the ideals of freedom and equality is evident in Rawls' use of the term reciprocity:

> The criterion of reciprocity requires that, when terms are proposed as the most reasonable terms of fair cooperation, those proposing them must think it at least reasonable for others to accept them, *as free and equal citizens*, and not as dominated or manipulated or under pressure caused by an inferior political or social position.[5] (*italics mine*)

Defined in this manner, the criterion of reciprocity draws on the ideals discussed so far. Each citizen has the power to affirm or deny a claim or proposal. Each citizen is free. Each citizen is also equal under the law: a government must follow the same procedures in its actions towards citizens; a government must respect the fact that all of its citizens are free. However, what the criterion of reciprocity adds to the ideals of consent and equality is the context of public debate. Political claims or proposals must satisfy the criterion of reciprocity. Reasoning must conform to basic moral standards in order to be public.

## Public Reason

The criterion of reciprocity identifies a quality of public speech and reasoning. Only proposals that meet the criterion of reciprocity can become a part of the constitution of a society. Likewise, the criminal and civil laws of society and the policies of government must conform to this standard.

Interpreted in this fashion, the criterion of reciprocity is primarily corrective. It rules certain claims out of political life.[6] The claim "men can vote but women cannot" violates the criterion of reciprocity. It does not treat men and women equally and is unlikely to gain the consent of women—if women are asked this question and are not "dominated or manipulated or under the pressure of an inferior political or social position."[7] Similarly, the claim "male children must receive a primary school education but female children should not" violates the criterion of reciprocity. It creates an arbitrary distinction between boys and girls and men and women—and it is unlikely to be accepted by women if their view of the matter is asked.

The corrective sense of this ideal is extraordinarily important. The criterion of reciprocity establishes a minimum moral condition of political speech. In this case, a state that fails to acknowledge the freedom and equality of women is not just to half of its citizens. It has created an underclass within the state.

The corrective aspect of the criterion of reciprocity does not separate morality and politics. In Rawls' account, a moral standard must enter into the formulation of laws and policy. But it is also important to avoid defining this ideal in too narrow a way. It is not simply examining the view of policy makers that is meant here. Rawls' conception encourages every citizen to make political proposals. Each citizen is a potential source of thought and policy in the life of a people.[8] Moreover, the kinds of proposals change when the needs and interests and beliefs of other people are kept in mind. The criterion of reciprocity fosters a mentality of participation and inclusion.

Thus, if women and men can vote, own property, receive an education and make political proposals—and men and women acknowledge the justice of these practices and seek to further them—a substantial change has occurred. In this situation, the criterion of reciprocity does more than balance the status of men and women in political life. It also makes possible new forms of relation. The attitudes of husband and wife are no longer hierarchical and are instead based on agreement or consent. The relation between parents and daughter also changes, since the mental life of girls is affirmed and trained. Women can run for office and, more generally, the concept of gender roles is diminished in society.

Seen in this light, the criterion of reciprocity affects some of the most basic habits of thought and life. The mentality of inclusion is very different from the mentality of exclusion.

## 2. DEMOCRATIC FOREIGN POLICY

Rawls places the ideals of freedom, equality and reciprocity at the center of a democratic regime: if all persons ask the question "What kind of society do I wish to belong to?" A possible answer could be: a regime in which the freedom and equality of all citizens is acknowledged and affirmed—and the beliefs of citizens are politically relevant.

This emphasis, however, is not simply abstract. Universal suffrage, a fair trial for all, mandatory education for all, ownership of property—these practices draw the ideals of freedom, equality and reciprocity into the daily workings of a society. In a liberal regime, the expression of coercive force is limited and constrained by its practices, not just its ideals.

I would now like to expand on Rawls' sense of a liberal regime by examining its foreign policy.[9] In Rawls' view, a foreign policy that seeks to dominate its neighbors is aggressive and unjust. Democratic foreign policy should not follow the path of political realism.

## Security

Rawls brings moral standards or ideals into the relation between nations; in Rawls' view, every democratic society must treat every other democratic society in a free, equal and reciprocal manner; a federation of democracies is created when these ideals and practices are widely accepted.[10]

Rawls calls the antithesis of this recommendation political realism. At the most basic level, political realism views the attempt to bring ideals into politics in a negative manner. From the point of view of political realism, idealism in the international domain undermines the security of a state.

## Security as Expansion

Why would a thinker dismiss the role of ideals in the relation between states? What arguments lie behind this doctrine or set of beliefs?

Here it might be useful to look at an earlier thinker in the social contract tradition—John Locke—and examine his approach to the relation between states. When Locke, in *A Letter Concerning Toleration*, speaks about the origin and goals of society, he says the following:

> But forasmuch as Men thus entering into Societies, grounded upon their mutual Compacts of Assistance, for the Defence of their Temporal Goods, may nevertheless be deprived of them, either by the Rapine and Fraud of their fellow citizens, or by the hostile violence of Forreignors; the Remedy of this evil consists in Arms, Riches, and Multitude of Citizens; the Remedy of the other in Laws . . .[11]

In this passage, basic assumptions in Locke's thought appear. Male persons—Locke's view is, indeed, sexist—enter into society for mutual protection.[12] That is, a society is formed when several males agree to follow basic rules the government enforces. Moreover, these rules are not exploitative for these male citizens. Instead, these rules or laws are meant to protect the body, the property, and the rights of every "Man." As Locke later says "The sum of all we drive at is, That every Man may enjoy the same Rights that are granted to others."[13]

For Locke, the rule of law is evident in the domestic domain. In the international domain, however, the situation is different. In this case, Locke does not speak of laws and basic or fundamental rights. Instead, Locke speaks of the need for "Arms, Riches, and a Multitude of Citizens." The international domain is a situation of perpetual hostility and calls for "Strength," not law.[14]

The division between the domestic case and the international case in Locke's thought is extraordinarily important and has far reaching consequences for policy and thought. In Locke's account, the main way to secure the body and property of citizens from the invasions of "forreignors" is to engage in an expansionist policy relative to other nations. The security of a state is achieved by increasing its strength.[15]

*Domestic Capture*

Locke—unlike Rawls—does not foresee a peaceful international system; in Locke's view, all societies are in a perpetual state of anarchy with each other. But the point I wish to make here is narrower in scope and centers on the effects of Locke's foreign policy on his domestic policy: in political realism, foreign policy captures domestic policy in several important respects.

Consider Locke's prescription for a "Multitude of Citizens." In order to increase the number of citizens in a state a government might 1) support the birth rate, or 2) reduce the mortality rate, or 3) encourage immigration. A state that wishes to increase the number of citizens can follow one—or some combination of—these "policies." And if one refines the goal of this policy to increase the number of young citizens—since young male citizens, presumably, are needed to fight in the army in the seventeenth century—Locke's prescription for "Arms" has substantial implications for the status of women and children. The birth rate must remain high and the health of children takes on political significance.[16]

A policy of population growth—to man a strong army—also has substantial implications for the domestic economic policies of a state. If the population is growing there are more citizens engaged in labor and work. Thus, a larger population of economically active citizens increases the "Riches" of the society and the tax base of its government.

Or, to refine this thought: it is not enough to simply have a large number of citizens engaged in labor and work. These citizens must be more productive than the citizens of other nations in order to adequately fund an army. If one state loses the economic race to another state—if a foreign state can accumulate more riches and thus spend more on its armed forces—the situation is threatening and undermines security.

From this point of view, a policy of "Strength" calls for an expansionist economic policy. It becomes a matter of national security or the public good to have the most productive economy.

A final comment is relevant here. A policy of population growth and economic growth greatly affect the life of men, women, and children in a state. There must be more citizens and these citizens must be productively employed—relative to other nations. But this is not all. These policies also have substantial implications for the land use practices of a state. In particular, an expansionist policy requires a decrease in wilderness—since it is unclear how a state in the seventeenth century can have more citizens, more riches, and a large and vigorous army relative to other nations without increasing the surface area of the earth it occupies and exploits. At the very least, more food is needed to feed a larger population and more natural resources are required to provide the materials and energy for a growing economy and army.

Seen in this light, the division between "citizens" and "forreignors" changes the terms of the social contract. Once the expansion of "Arms," "Riches" and "Citizens"—relative to other nations—is adopted as the ultimate goal of government, there are major implications for domestic policy. Expansion in the name of security changes the relationship between citizens, government and the earth.

*War*

Political realism affects the internal structure of a society. Foreign policy, far from being separate from domestic policy, in fact boomerangs back to control domestic policy in several critical respects.

I would now like to turn to some of the effects of political realism on the relation between nations. The policy of strength may invoke the security of the state as its ultimate justification. But does the policy of strength actually achieve the goal of security from foreign threats? What are the short and long term consequences of this policy?

Consider economic expansion again. In political realism, the citizens of one's own nation must be more productive than the citizens of other nations. But it is unclear how this goal can be achieved without placing the labor and work of one's own citizens ahead of the labor and work of "forreignors."

From this point of view, an expansionist economic policy can easily shade into mercantilism; if the labor and work of one's own citizens must always surpass the labor and work of "forreignors," the protection of one's own economy becomes paramount. In this case, the citizens of one's own nation become a kind of permanent economic upperclass relative to the citizens of other nations. "Citizens" have higher status than "forreignors" in the trade policies of government.

The policy of protecting the economic activity of one's citizens—at the expense of the citizens of other nations—is a form of economic nationalism.[17] It involves the privileging of one's own civilians above all others. But now consider the thought process of neighboring heads of state in this situation. If one nation adopts a mercantilist policy what should other heads of state do? Should they do nothing? Or should the heads of other states adopt protectionist measures to support the labor and work of their own citizens? What head of state is likely to consent to permanent membership in an economic underclass?

Here, a pitfall of political realism comes into view. One problem with political realism is its inability to factor in the predictable consequences of "realist" policy. What happens when many nations adopt a mercantilist policy at the same time? What happens if many nations privilege their own citizens at the expense of "forreignors"?

This criticism can be sharpened. As noted earlier, economic expansion in Locke's thought is interdependent with many other factors. In Locke's view, population growth, higher food production and more natural resources and territory are needed to fuel economic expansion—thereby increasing the strength of one's nation. But what happens when a nation's territory becomes insufficient and can no longer sustain the demands of an expansionist economy? Won't the eyes of government begin to gaze out towards other lands and people?

From this point of view, a policy of strength can easily blend into a policy of colonialism and empire. And it is important to acknowledge that Locke was one the many architects of England's expansion into a global power in the seventeenth century.[18]

Here again, however, one must step back and examine the short and long term consequences of this policy. A head of state might pursue an expansionist policy in the name of security. However, a policy of expansion does not occur in a vacuum. Others are always watching. And what should these other heads of state do when they see their rival expanding its territory, riches and arms? Should these onlooking heads of state do nothing? Or should they follow suit and seek to expand? The chances are high these onlooking heads of state will follow suit. As Machiavelli would say: "a prince" must "learn to be able not to be good" in order to "maintain himself."[19]

At this point, the problem inherent in political realism turns into a cavern—or a bottomless pit. If several governments simultaneously adopt the policy of expanding their strength and territory in the name of security, the inevitable result is conflict between states and a globe full of oppressed peoples. The cruelty and misery justified in the name of political realism is staggeringly large.[20]

Understood in this way, political realism involves a monumental tradeoff. The policy of expansion can achieve some measure of strength. But this policy also leads to a situation Rawls calls "global anarchy," as states vie with each other to become stronger and more powerful.[21]

### Repetition

The pitfalls of political realism are very clear to Rawls. The policy of strength—when followed by several states—inevitably leads to conflict between these states. And, in truth, it does not take several states to create this situation. As Rawls observes: "One strong state possessed of military and economic power and embarked on expansion and glory is sufficient to perpetuate the cycle of war and preparation for war."[22] A single expansionist state is enough to trigger the anxiety of its neighbors.

From this point of view, one can understand why Rawls believes new ideals and practices are needed in the international domain. Something other than political realism must come to define the relation between nations—if the cycle of war and preparation for war is to be broken.

### Other Paths

As noted before, Rawls does not believe conflict and war between nations is inevitable or a matter of fate: Rawls believes a future free of conflict and war is possible on the earth. The question of the security of a people, however, remains. How will a democratic regime defend itself?

The broad outlines of Rawls' response are as follows. It is a mistake to assume that all regimes everywhere are hostile to each other; in the contemporary world, a very, very small number of regimes are expansionist or preparing to expand. Democratic societies, on the other hand, are not threats to each other. From an empirical and historical point of view, stable democracies do not go to war *with each other*.[23]

Rawls' first response to the problem of security, then, is to more carefully define the sense of a threat. Instead of anxiety about all peoples everywhere, anxiety is replaced by what one might call "an evidence-based fear" of outlaw regimes. Undifferentiated anxiety towards all peoples everywhere — a core assumption of political realism — can easily lead to the belief that war is eternal.

The second feature of Rawls response builds on the first. Democracies are not threats to each other. On the contrary, democracies should *ally* with each other in peace and in wars of defense.[24] The foreign policy of the different democracies of the world can be coordinated together. And this is not a minor point. It is very significant. Mutually beneficial trade and the joint use of force greatly enhance the security of the world's democracies. Much can be accomplished by acting together.

*The Second World War*

So far, I have described Rawls' foreign policy through a series of contrasts. Britain, Spain, France and other nations pursued colonies around the world in the sixteenth and seventeenth centuries. The "Great Game" continued to be played well into the twentieth century. The ideal democracy, however does not seek to expand its territory through invasion and conquest. The ideal democracy is not an expansionist regime.

Rawls contrasts the ideal democracy with states that seek colonies. Conquering another people is not something the ideal democracy will ever do. However, Rawls also speaks about the states that initiated World War II. He offers lengthy assessments of the Nazi regime of Germany and the Tojo regime of Japan. And while these states shared many similarities with the colonial states of the early modern period there are also features of Hitler's regime in particular that made it distinctively horrific. There are new forms of violence at work here.

Rawls analysis of Hitler's regime is split in two. He treats the foreign policy and the domestic policy of this state in separate places. That is, Rawls evaluates the Holocaust and the German regime's apparent desire for global control.[25] But at the root of both discussions is the incredible power the regime had to achieve its deranged objectives. As Rawls notes, "nowhere, other than German-occupied Europe between 1941 and 1945, has a charismatic dictator controlled the machinery of a powerful state so focused on carrying out the final and complete extermination of a people, hitherto regarded as members of society."[26] The combination of extreme powers and deranged goals led to the murder of many millions of persons. Rawls notes that "People of all ages, the elderly, children and infants, were treated the same."[27]

Recent studies indicate that the Holocaust was even larger than previously estimated.[28] A powerful modern state with a policy of murder can accomplish its goals with industrial efficiency. The *machinery* of murder is the term Rawls invokes. But Rawls also notes that Hitler's regime was focused on expansion in the most radical sense of this word. The world state—or something like it—seems to have been the final objective. And while the fortunes of war turned against the Nazi regime in 1942, one can imagine what would have happened in Britain and the Soviet Union had the German state accomplished its immediate goal of conquering these nations.[29] In Rawls' view an expansionist regime like Hitler's state must be stopped.

## Nuclear Deterrence

*The Law of Peoples* offers a description of two time frames of very extreme expansionist ambition. The European colonial period and the regimes that initiated World War II are recurring themes in this text. And while the ideal democracy does not use state power to advance its interests Rawls is also aware of the potential strength of outlaw regimes. Rawls makes references to the military strategy of democratic societies throughout *The Law of Peoples*.

The first part of this strategy has already been described. Rawls believes democratic and decent societies can align with each other when it comes to issues of trade and national defense. Collective *international* action can provide more security to the world's peoples. However, Rawls is not certain these policies by themselves will achieve the necessary military strength to deter outlaw regimes. And so he goes beyond the discussion of trade and alliances and claims that the ideal democracy must maintain a nuclear arsenal.[30] By possessing nuclear weapons, the ideal democracy can avoid a situation of excessive military weakness relative to expansionist states. The threat of a nuclear reprisal will ultimately deter outlaw regimes.

## Proliferation

The overall argument of *The Law of Peoples* has now come into view. And while Rawls rules expansionist wars entirely out of the picture his discussion of national defense leads him very far afield. At one moment, he speaks of communicating human rights to the civilian populations of outlaw regimes *during* a war. A few pages later, he speaks of targeting civilians in times of "Supreme Emergency," and indicates that Britain in the early stages of World War II—from 1939 to early 1942—could have acted in this manner. There is an incredibly large shift in perspective here.[31]

Rawls is willing to justify a great deal to hold outlaw regimes at bay. Rawls' foreign policy points in two very different directions. And it is this split perspective that I wish to carefully examine in this text. Rawls is trying to introduce an alternative way of thinking about international relations in *The Law of Peoples*. Something other than global anarchy needs to govern the states of the world. The point Rawls makes here is of lasting significance. I think, however, that Rawls' endorsement of nuclear deterrence sets in motion problems of its own. As Sen notes, the construction of a single nuclear weapon is an act of incredible hostility. It gives heads of state the ability to kill hundreds of thousands of civilians in an instant. The detonation of a nuclear weapon can make the mountains "turn white."[32] But as Sen also notes, one state's power to destroy is not all that is at issue here. The construction of a single nuclear weapon can push other heads of state to pursue this power. The construction of a single nuclear weapon leads to nuclear proliferation and very dangerous conflict spirals. Is a world in which many nations possess a nuclear arsenal really the best strategy of national defense?

From this point of view, Rawls' claim that the ideal democracy must possess nuclear weapons—to keep outlaw regimes at bay—requires more scrutiny than Rawls provides. The *ideal* democracy may not be interpreted as threatening to its neighbors. But the history of nuclear weapons after World War II is one of proliferation. More and more actually exist-

ing states have developed "the bomb." But even this historical observation understates the case. In the absence of a global framework for nuclear disarmament—which is a primary goal of Sen's foreign policy—additional states may choose the path of nuclear weapons in the future. It
does not take much to see where all of this is heading.

Understood in this way, a very careful analysis of the goals of foreign
policy—an analysis of the kind that Rawls and Sen both provide—is an
extremely urgent matter. It is, ultimately, for this reason that I have
brought together a discussion of the foreign policies of Rawls and Sen.

## SUMMARY

Reviewing the claims of this section, one can say the following:

1. Locke distinguishes between the domestic policy of a state and the
   foreign policy of a state. Domestic policy calls for rights and the
   rule of law. Foreign policy calls for "Strength."
2. In Locke's account, more citizens, a more productive economy,
   more territory and a strong army are needed—relative to other
   nations—to achieve political strength.
3. Locke distinguishes between domestic and foreign policy. However, domestic and foreign policy are in fact inextricably linked. A
   policy of strength changes the relations between citizens, their
   government and the earth.
4. In Rawls' view, a federation of democratic and decent regimes
   provides a people with stability and security as well as the institutions of justice. Rawls departs from the policies of political realism.
5. In Rawls' analysis, a society must avoid excessive military weakness, relative to the expansionist states of their time. In Rawls'
   view, the possesion of nuclear weapons deters outlaw regimes
   from expansionist wars.

The Domestic Social Contract

elect representatives,
accept the laws passed by
elected representatives

civilians ⟶ representatives +
the armed forces

protect the rights of civilians,
promote the public good
through legislation

The International Social Contract

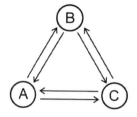

Each society is free and equal.

## NOTES

1. "My aim is to present a conception of justice that generalizes and carries to a higher level of abstraction the familiar theory of a social contract as found, say, in Locke, Rousseau and Kant." Rawls, *A Theory of Justice*, 10. See also Rawls, *The Law of Peoples*, 4.

2. Locke places the ideal of consent at the center of his political philosophy: "Men being, as has been said, by Nature, free, equal and independent, no one can be put out of his Estate, and subjected to the Political Power of another, without his own Consent." John Locke, *Two Treatises of Government*, 330. The identification of consent with an election is also a feature of Locke's thought. As Richard Ashcraft notes: "In a well-ordered or 'Constituted Commonwealth,' Locke insists that there is a continuous connection between the people and their government maintained through the medium of elections, whereby the people give their consent to laws enacted by their deputies or representatives." Richard Ashcraft, "Locke's Political Theory" in *The Cambridge Companion to Locke*, edited by Vere Chappell, 232.

3. Rawls, *Justice as Fairness: A Restatement*, 17.

4. " . . . we must specify a point of view from which a fair agreement between free and equal persons can be reached." Rawls, *Justice as Fairness: A Restatement*, 17.

5. Rawls, *The Law of Peoples*, 14.

6. Ibid., 137-138.

7. Ibid., 138. See also Rawls, *Justice and Fairness: A Restatement*, 166: "The equal rights of women and the claims of their children as future citizens are inalienable and

protect them wherever they are . . . gender distinctions limiting those rights and liberties are excluded."

8. Rawls, *The Law of Peoples*, 137. The Kantian echoes of this point are very clear: " . . . every rational being must so act as if he were through his maxim always *a legislating member* in a universal kingdom of ends." (*italics mine*) Kant, *Grounding for the Metaphysics of Morals*, 43.

9. Rawls, *The Law of Peoples*, 10.

10. Rawls, *The Law of Peoples*, 4.

11. Locke, *A Letter Concerning Toleration*, 47-48. J. R. Milton notes that the "immediate impetus" for Locke's composition of *A Letter Concerning Toleration* seems to have been "the revocation of the Edict of Nantes in 1685." J. R. Milton, "Locke's Life and Times" in *The Cambridge Companion to Locke*, edited by Vere Chappell, 16.

12. There are many passages in Locke's writing that diminish women. For instance, in *Two Treatises on Government*, one can find the following claim: "But the Husband and Wife, though they have but one common Concern, yet have different understandings, will unavoidably sometimes have different wills too; it therefore being necessary, that the last Determination, i.e. the Rule, should be placed somewhere, it naturally falls to the Man's share, as the abler and stronger." Locke, *Two Treatises of Government*, 321.

13. Locke, *A Letter Concerning Toleration*, 53.

14. "Provision may be made for the security of each Man's private Possessions . . . and, as much as possible, for the Increase of their inward Strength, against foreign invasions." Ibid., 48.

15. For more on the colonial dimension of Locke's thought see Barbara Arneil's *John Locke and America: The Defense of English Colonialism*: "The development of natural-law theory . . . was firmly rooted in the colonial expansion of Spain, Holland, and England. Grotius and Locke used natural law to reach positions justifying their country's claims in disputes over colonization in the new world." In particular, the theory of property defended in *Two Treatises of Government* gives English citizens ownership rights over Native American lands: "Because land cultivation in common cannot be considered appropriated or of any value until it is enclosed by the individual, Amerindians engaged in agricultural activities as a collective unit, rather than as individuals within enclosed ground, will have no exclusive right to their property. Thus, the aboriginal nation, in Locke's theory of property, can have no authority over their land, until it adopts a European form of agrarian labor. Title to property—that is, the right to exclude it from others—can only be claimed, by definition, by the individual." Barbara Arneil, *John Locke and America: The Defense of English Colonialism*, 135, 141.

16. Locke, *A Letter Concerning Toleration*, 40. For more discussion of Locke's treatment of public health, see chapter 3.

17. "Mercantilists were economic nationalists who believed that economic policy was an instrument of state policy for the promotion of state interests, and that the state should regulate trade with that aim in mind . . . With respect to foreign policy, mercantilist policies aimed to strengthen the power of the state against other states in the system." Jack S. Levy and William R. Thompson, *Causes of War*, 70.

18. "Locke was not only interested in the ideas but deeply immersed in the development of actual colonial policy as secretary to the Lords Proprietors of Carolina from 1668-1675, through his work for the 1672-1676 Council of Trade, and as Commissioner for the Board of Trade and Plantations from 1695-1700. In each of these capacities, he played an important role in formulating the policies to be implemented . . . There is

considerable evidence of the extent to which colonial policy dominated Locke's life from 1668-1675. From the colonial records of Carolina, one can see that most of the letters between the Lord Proprietors and the Council in Carolina were endorsed by Locke, some of the laws, including the Temporary Laws of 1674, were handwritten and sent by him, and copious notes summarizing the activities were recorded in his own hand. In addition, he wrote to senior officials in the colonies of the Bahamas and Carolina, including Joseph West, Peter Colleton, and Henry Woodward of his own accord during this time. Finally, he was responsible, in conjunction with Shaftesbury, for penning the Fundamental Constitutions of Carolina." Barbara Arneil, *John Locke and America: The Defence of English Colonialism*, 88-89.

19. "For a man who wants to make a profession of good in all regards must come to ruin among so many who are not good. Hence it is necessary to a prince, if he wants to maintain himself, to learn to be able not to be good, and to use this and not use it according to necessity." Machiavelli, *The Prince*, 61.

20. Levy and Thompson note that mercantilism was explicitly framed in terms of colonialism: "Mercantilist economic ideology led to closed trading systems, not open, liberal, free—trading systems. Most of a state's trade was conducted with its own colonies, not with competitors, who were excluded from a state's economic sphere. State leaders feared that trade with competitors would only enrich their adversaries and increase their long-term military power and potential. The closed trading systems of the mercantilist were significantly different than the free trading systems that emerged with liberal economic systems." Jack S. Levy and William R. Thompson, *Causes of War*, 70.

21. Rawls, *The Law of Peoples*, 27-28.

22. Ibid., 48.

23. Ibid., 8, 52. Rawls also notes exceptions to this claim. These exceptions are discussed in the final chapter.

24. Ibid., 54.

25. Ibid.,19-23, 98-99.

26. Rawls, *The Law of Peoples*, 20.

27. Ibid., 20.

28. Geoffrey Megargee and Martin Dean now estimate that 15 to 20 million persons died or were imprisoned in the Holocaust. See also Eric Lichtblau, "The Holocaust Just Got More Shocking" published in the *New York Times*. http://www.nytimes.com/2013/03/03/sunday-review/the-holocaust-just-got-more-shocking.html?pagewanted=allr;=0

29. Rawls notes that Hitler's invasion of the Soviet Union was aimed at the elimination of Slavic peoples—with the remnant population reduced to the status of serfs. Rawls, *The Law of Peoples*, 99.

30. Rawls, *The Law of Peoples*, 9.

31. Compare 96 with 98 and 99 of *The Law of Peoples*.

32. Sen, *The Argumentative Indian*, 256.

# 1

# Domestic Policy

# ONE

## Interaction

The critique of political realism is a defining moment in *The Law of Peoples*. Political realism fails to take into account the predictable consequences of "realist" policy and can lead in the worst cases to new conflicts and war. Widespread hostility and suspicion—and a globe full of oppressed peoples—are likely outcomes of realist policy.

Interpreted in this manner, political realism is not only an immoral doctrine. It also makes a very fundamental intellectual error. A key deficiency of political realism is an accurate picture of how states *interact*. A state might believe it is increasing its security by increasing its strength. But when one nation increases its military power, an adjacent state might adopt a similar strategy. Who wants to fall into a condition of military weakness relative to their expansionist neighbor? And since the world consists of many states—not just two—this type of reasoning can become widespread and tends to reinforce itself. Several states can simultaneously adopt the goal of expanding their power.

Viewed from this broader perspective, the policy of security through expansion actually intensifies the condition of global anarchy. It creates a general climate of hostility and suspicion that makes war more likely. And one must remember that Rawls is not only thinking about colonialism in this context. He is also thinking about the two World Wars.[1] States cannot be thought of as isolated entities. States are a part of a larger system.

Rawls' critique of political realism is both moral and intellectual. Political realism is cruel and fails to understand the predictable consequences of realist policy. Rawls offers a comprehensive rebuttal of this theory. However, what is distinctive about *The Law of Peoples* is Rawls' response to these problems. By replacing global anarchy with the rule of law a less hostile international system can be created. The title of Rawls' book—*The Law of Peoples*—is the name Rawls gives to a possible system of stabilizing international rules.[2]

Rawls seeks to replace a framework of global anarchy with a fair system of cooperation. The stability provided by the rule of law is more just and more effective than the largest army. But what I would like to do now is take a step back and reflect on the relationship between *The Law of Peoples* and Rawls' earlier text *A Theory of Justice*. I will also say a few words about the novel arguments within *The Law of Peoples* relative to Rawls' earlier work.

## 1. JUST WAR

Rawls' book *A Theory of Justice* was first published in 1971 and focused on the construction of a single ideal society, using the thought experiment of the social contract to advance the argument. Reflections on foreign policy are mostly limited to sections 56 through 58 of this text and arise because of Rawls' interest in civil disobedience and conscientious refusal. Rawls also speaks at some length about pacifism in these sections.

I am not going to present an extended interpretation of *A Theory of Justice* but I think Rawls' intention in writing these sections is clear. It is one thing to agree to join a hypothetical society. But the question of allegiance to actual states is something else entirely. What stance should a person take up towards their society if it possesses some features of justice but also affirms terrible and cruel practices—such as holding persons as slaves? This is Thoreau's problem in his essay *Civil Disobedience*—which Rawls cites.[3] But Rawls also takes up this question in regards to the *foreign* policy of states. What should a person do if the state they are born into possesses some features of just institutions but is also pursuing a radically unjust foreign policy? Can a person refuse military service in this situation?

Interpreted in this manner, sections 56 through 58 are primarily concerned with *an individual's* stance towards the law and policies *of their own state*. What are the obligations of a citizen in this mixed—and very confusing—situation? However, in the context of this discussion Rawls is pushed to make a number of claims about a just foreign policy. And this is where the overlap between *A Theory of Justice* and *The Law of Peoples* begins to appear. For instance, in section 58 of *A Theory of Justice* Rawls claims that:

> A nation will aim above all to maintain and to preserve its just institutions and the conditions that make them possible. It is not moved by the desire for world power or national glory; nor does it wage war for purposes of economic gain or the acquisition of territory. These ends are contrary to the conception of justice that defines a society's legitimate interests, however prevalent they have been in the actual conduct of states.[4]

This passage hones in on *the motives* of the state at war. *If* a state is fighting a war of self-defense—to protect its institutions and its people from an aggressive neighbor—the war is just. *If,* on the other hand, the motive of the state is to expand its territory or gain the natural resources of a colony or to seek glory or world power the war is unjust. The intentions that motivate the decision to go to war distinguish wars from each other.

In Rawls' account, the justice of a war depends on the motives that set the war in motion. Acquiring territory, economic gain, a desire for glory or the delusional fantasy of world control: none of these objectives count as appropriate reasons to invade one's neighbor. Only wars of self-defense are legitimate. Moreover, the kind of war that is being fought has implications for the decision to refuse military service. A citizen cannot refuse military service if the state they belong to is fighting a just war of self-defense. Rawls does not defend conscientious refusal in this situation. An expansionist war, however, is a different situation. *If* the state unleashes the horrors of war to gain power and territory, a refusal of military service is a justifiable decision.

Rawls presents the kernel of the just war doctrine he will develop in *The Law of Peoples* in the passage on conscientious refusal. States cannot use war to advance their power—and citizens do not have to support unjust wars through their own military service. The critique of political realism is in evidence here.

Rawls indicts expansionist wars in *A Theory of Justice* and *The Law of Peoples*. The core foreign policy argument of both texts is the same. A second feature of Rawls' discussion in *A Theory of Justice* that is germane to *The Law of Peoples* is his theory of conscription. In particular, Rawls claims that: "Conscription is permissible only if it is demanded for the defense of liberty itself, including here not only the liberties of the citizens of societies in question, but also those of other societies as well."[5] What is Rawls saying here?

On one level, the quote reinforces Rawls' views about a just war. Conscription is permissible when the existence of a society is directly threatened by an expansionist state. A war of national defense justifies conscription. Rawls, however, also makes reference to conscription to protect *other societies* in this passage. The notion of a *protective alliance*— between non-expansionist nations—is affirmed.

From this point of view, a second key element of *The Law of Peoples* is present in *A Theory of Justice*. Rawls is thinking about an international *system* of national defense. At no point was Rawls an isolationist in his thinking about foreign policy.

*Resignation*

So far, this review of *A Theory of Justice* has revealed two features of Rawls' foreign policy that carry over into *The Law of Peoples*. The criticism of political realism is evident. Rawls also stresses the need for non-expansionist states to assist each other in wars of defense. No society—and here one might think of Britain in 1939—should be forced to go it alone against an outlaw regime.

Rawls does not believe just or decent states should stand alone in the international system. Withdrawal from the international stage is not Rawls' ideal. A third feature of sections 56 through 58 I would like to highlight involves the more subtle elements of resignation and pacifism in Rawls' discussion. These are also important and lasting parts of Rawls' foreign policy in my view.

For instance, Rawls notes that conscription and the exposure to war are made necessary by hostile states: "in a well-ordered society . . . these evils arise externally, that is, from unjustified attacks from the outside."[6] The draft—and the burdens of war—is one way an expansionist society distorts a liberal regime. But this is not all. Rawls also claims that: "it is impossible for just institutions to eliminate these hardships entirely."[7] Wars that threaten the existence of society are always possible, and thus the suffering occasioned by wars cannot be prevented. The ideal society of *A Theory of Justice* is unable to avoid the severe wounds and death inevitably caused by the conscription of citizens.

Rawls does not seem overly optimistic about the ability of the ideal society to transcend war. The picture is one in which the draft is always possible. But this is not the only element of resignation in *A Theory of Justice*. There are a number of very skeptical comments about strong states in these sections.

For instance, Rawls claims that: "the conduct and aims of states in waging war, *especially large and powerful ones*, are in some circumstances so likely to be unjust that one is forced to conclude that in the foreseeable future one must abjure military service altogether." (*italics mine*)[8] The militarily powerful states are very often aggressors—while the less powerful states are often the victims in international relations.

Rawls draws attention to the asymmetries of the international system in regards to military power. Some states are much stronger than other states in the world. The size, organization and lethality of the armies of the globe are not the same. But it is not just the existence of military asymmetry that Rawls singles out here. It is the way militarily stronger states *use* this asymmetry that is so unjust. It is the militarily powerful states of the world that initiate expansionist wars. The perception of military weakness is a critical problem in international relations.

Rawls' most skeptical statement about existing states is presented in this context. He notes—as if it were an obvious fact—that military stronger states often see military weaker states not as potential allies in need of assistance but as possible targets of an expansionist war: "Given the often predatory aims of state power," Rawls says at one point.[9] The tendency of powerful states to misuse their power is very clear to Rawls.

### Contingent Pacifism

The passages on state power reveal Rawls' distance from the foreign policy of actual nations. The world is filled with aggressive states. And this sets the stage for Rawls' first mention of the social contract in the international sphere. Instead of using its military power to get what it wants, the ideal democracy cannot appeal to the size of its army when negotiating with peaceful societies. The ideal democracy cannot draw on its knowledge of "its power and strength in comparison with other nations."[10]

On the ideal level, Rawls approach to the perception of militarily weaker states is to rule this perception out of negotiation. The international social contract, Rawls says, "nullifies the contingencies and biases of historical fate."[11] But, as was noted before, the perspective of sections 56 through 58 is not only the perspective of ideal theory. Rawls is also speaking about the stance individuals take up towards the foreign policy of their own societies. How can individuals *transition* the foreign policy of their own regimes? How can persons make the foreign policy of their own society a little better? And it is within this context that Rawls makes a number of very sympathetic comments about pacifism. In a key passage, Rawls states:

> The political principles recognized by the community have a certain affinity with the doctrine the pacifist professes. *There is a common abhorrence with war and the use of force,* and a belief in the equal status of men as moral persons. And given the tendency of nations, particularly great powers, to engage in war unjustifiably and to set in motion the apparatus of the state to suppress dissent, *the respect accorded to pacifism serves the purpose of alerting citizens to the wrongs that governments are prone to commit in their name.* (italics mine)[12]

In this passage, pacifism stands against the tendency of rulers to use war to advance state power. It is a form of *public* argument that resists—in a nonviolent manner—the political realism of actually existing heads of state.

## Conduct of War

Rawls expresses skepticism about militarily strong states in *A Theory of Justice*. Militarily strong states are likely to invoke the size of their armies in their negotiations and decisions. The reasoning of a militarily strong state can be fundamentally warped—and is very much in need of publicly reasoned resistance. The last topic I would like to address in this review of *A Theory of Justice* is Rawls' thoughts about the *conduct* of a just war of self-defense. How can the ideal society defend itself?

As discussed in the introduction, Rawls offers clear answers to this question in *The Law of Peoples*. He notes that the ideal democracy must possess nuclear weapons to deter outlaw states. He also notes that the civilians of an outlaw regime can be targeted in a supreme emergency—when the existence of a democracy is directly threatened. However, in *A Theory of Justice*, the situation is a little harder to read. Rawls references nuclear weapons only once in this text. In particular, Rawls cites the text *Nuclear Weapons and Christian Conscience*—published in 1965, three years after the Cuban Missile Crisis—as an example of a critical stance an *indi-*

*vidual* can take up towards nuclear war as a strategy of defense. A just war, the authors argue, cannot involve the total destruction of human life on the planet. A form of pacifism—in regards to nuclear war—is affirmed. And while Rawls himself does not explicitly identify nuclear war in the main body of *A Theory of Justice*, he does make the following statement: "The aim of war is a just peace, and therefore the means employed must not destroy the possibility of peace *or encourage a contempt for human life that puts the safety of ourselves and mankind in jeopardy*."(italics mine)[13]

In this quote, Rawls makes the same argument the authors of *Nuclear Weapons and Christian Conscience* make. Any strategy that is based on "assured destruction" is not a just strategy of national defense. The means pursued in national defense cannot end humanity or put humanity as a whole at risk. In this way Rawls shows his distance from the policies of the Cold War—and the rapid construction of thousands of nuclear weapons that took place during this period.[14]

## *Truman*

The strategy of "assured destruction" is fundamentally flawed to Rawls. Any strategy of defense that actively embraces nuclear war is a terrible mistake. But can a society use a single nuclear weapon in a just war of self-defense? Does Rawls make any comments about this question in *A Theory of Justice*?

On this point *A Theory of Justice* is silent. But when Walter Stein—in the introductory essay to *Nuclear Weapons and Christian Conscience*—argues against the use of nuclear weapons, he frames his point in the following way:

> Suppose a raid is aimed directly at the houses and hospitals or schools of a city, or is to cover a centre of population so extensively that military and non-military targets are indiscriminately affected, there can no longer be any justification in terms of "double effect." Even if one allowed that the criterion of reasonable proportion might be satisfied; even if one could hold on to the notion of "unintended effects" in view of the massiveness of the circumstances involved: there can be no getting around the fact that these evils would be directly aimed at. Whatever the ultimate aim (i.e., victory for a just cause), the immediate aim would include the deliberate destruction of non-combatants—would include a commitment to mass murder.[15]

The conclusion Stein draws from this line of reasoning is stark: "This is why nuclear warfare is immoral." It kills non-combatants, who are innocent, and have no role in fighting the war.

The argument Stein provides in this passage is categorical. There is simply never any justification for this action—even if the supposed rationale is Truman's rationale of "victory for a just cause."[16] And what is true for Stein is true for Rawls in *The Law of Peoples*. According to Rawls, Truman's use of the atomic bomb in Hiroshima and Nagasaki ended the lives of thousands of civilians. These persons were infants and children, brothers and sisters, mothers and fathers, parents and grandparents, not involved in the war. They were innocent persons and had nothing to do with the decisions of the Tojo regime.

Stein and Rawls are in agreement about the decisions Truman took in August of 1945. Neither thinker affirmed Truman's choice. But one must be careful here. Stein and Rawls both criticize Truman. However, the reasons for this judgment are not quite the same. For Rawls, Truman's decision was not categorically or absolutely wrong. It was wrong because it targeted civilians *when there was no condition of supreme emergency*. In Rawls' view, the war against the Tojo regime was basically over—and the existence of democracy was not at stake at the time the atomic bombs were dropped on these two cities.[17]

Interpreted in this manner, Rawls adds an extra condition to the Catholic doctrines of war in *The Law of Peoples*. Rawls and Stein's views are similar. But they are *not* the same. Rawls leaves open the possibility of targeting civilians in a supreme emergency. And while Rawls does not present the case for nuclear weapons in *A Theory of Justice* the fact that he does not argue for nuclear disarmament is very revealing. Assured destruction is incompatible with a just policy of national defense. This is all Rawls says in *A Theory of Justice*.

### A Third Way

This review of *A Theory of Justice* has brought to light several claims. The foreign policy of an ideal democracy shares an affinity with pacifism in that it abhors war. However, this abhorrence of war does not mean the ideal democracy is unwilling to wage war. Wars of self-defense are necessary in Rawls' view. Defensive alliances between non-expansionist states are necessary. And while Rawls does not explicitly rule out the use of nuclear weapons in *A Theory of Justice* his reference to the contingent pacifism of Stein, G. E. M Anscombe, and others is very revealing. Rawls' thoughts about nuclear weapons are very far removed from the policies of Truman, Stalin, Eisenhower, Kennedy and Khruschev.

Interpreted in this manner, the ambiguity in Rawls' thinking about nuclear weapons is a longstanding feature of his foreign policy. Both *The Law of Peoples* and *A Theory of Justice* indicate a third way in regards to nuclear weapons—one that stands between disarmament and the aggressive postures adopted by actual heads of state. More generally, I find a great deal of overlap between sections 13 and 14 of *The Law of Peoples* and sections 56 through 58 of *A Theory of Justice*. There is no *significant* variation of argument here. Rawls' description of a just war, his insistence on alliances of defense, and his attempt to transition the policy of actual states away from political realism are all present in sections 56 through 58 of *A Theory of Justice*. Even Rawls' engagement with Catholic doctrines of war—including the doctrine of double effect and the claim that innocent civilians can never be targeted—is referenced in both works. These kernels of Rawls' foreign policy remained remarkably consistent.

## 2. CAUSES OF WAR

So far, I have been focusing on the line of argument that unites *A Theory of Justice* with *The Law of Peoples*. I would now like to reverse the perspective a bit and ask: what does *The Law of Peoples* add to *A Theory of Justice*? What new claims are presented in Rawls' more recent work?

As noted earlier, a key feature of *A Theory of Justice* is its description of state power. The strong states are most likely to engage in an expansionist war. However, these statements are basically assertions that Rawls makes no attempt to explain or interpret. The word "given"—as in the phrase "*Given* the often predatory nature of state power"—is repeated more than once.[18] But part of what Rawls tries to do in *The Law of Peoples* is to explain some of the factors that *cause* a state to pursue an expansionist policy. Rawls is especially focused on the *class structure* of these states. He claims that an outlaw regime's highly unequal class structure makes it more likely to engage in war.[19]

From this point of view, *The Law of Peoples* makes a new argument about the causes of war. In particular, Rawls argues that an *international system* of *highly stratified* states set the stage for colonialism and the two world wars. When ten or more powerful, extremely hierarchical, expansionist states share a continent, the end result is not very good.

## The Ideal Democracy Reconsidered

Rawls' identifies a connection between a society's class structure and the decision of its rulers to go to war. The way a state is organized predisposes that state to invade their neighbors. And this is an argument that does not arise in Rawls' earlier works. *A Theory of Justice*—as well as Rawls' later text *Political Liberalism*—makes no attempt to describe the internal structure of an outlaw regime. Nor did these texts seek to describe the interaction between different outlaw regimes. From this point of view, the argument in *The Law of Peoples* is unique within Rawls' corpus.

Rawls' hypothesis about the cause of war is very specific. Extreme inequality—*within a large number of powerful states*—is a leading cause of unjust war. But this new argument is not an isolated thesis within the text. Rawls' theory about the causes of war has ripple effects. It changes the way other parts of Rawls' argument are framed. In particular, Rawls' discussion of the ideal democracy in *The Law of Peoples* takes on an added dimension in this work. The internal organization of the ideal democracy makes it less likely to wage an unjust war.

From this point of the view, the ideal democracy in *The Law of Peoples* gains a second characterization. It provides justice to its citizens without threatening others. The internal structure of the ideal democracy makes it unlikely to expand. Moreover, an *international system* of liberal and decent societies—where each society lacks the highly unequal class structures of the early modern state—creates the possibility of a lasting peace.[20] A framework of trust and mutual goodwill between nations can develop, replacing the hostility and suspicion of earlier periods.

## Conscription and Elections

*The Law of Peoples* makes two arguments that are unique within Rawls' corpus. The first is a class-based analysis of an outlaw regime. The second is a class-based argument for international stability. And it is clear that both of these ideas are linked together in Rawls' thinking. The ideal democracy is the antithesis of the outlaw regime. But why, exactly, is Rawls confident about the peaceful character of the ideal society? What is the guiding intuition here?

Consider a point Rawls makes about conscription in *A Theory of Justice*:

> The most it can do is to try to make sure that the risks of suffering from these imposed misfortunes are more or less evenly shared by all members of society over the course of their life, *and that there is no avoidable class bias in selecting those who are called for duty.*[21] (*italics mine*)

In this passage, Rawls' primarily concern is an issue of fairness. A system of military conscription that draws only from impoverished or less well-off members of society is radically unjust. It has created an underclass within the state in regards to the hardships of war. But in *The Law of Peoples*, this idea takes on a second dimension. When the draft draws from all persons in society, regardless of class—and thus all members of society are confronted with the grim realities of war, either directly or through the experience of family members—the attitude of the citizenry in regards to entering war is likely to be much more cautious. The political culture of this society is more averse to unnecessary war.

Interpreted in this manner, a fair draft creates a very broad, shared sense of the burdens of war. *All* families are touched by the specter of conflict. And since the ideal society is a democracy—and its civilian population *elects* representatives—this shared sense of the burdens of war can inform each citizen's voting decisions.[22] It can make the citizenry less likely to vote for candidates seeking their own personal glory and fame.[23]

*Reciprocity and Foreign Policy*

Elections and a fair draft show how the internal structure of the ideal democracy can affect its foreign policy. The way a society is structured helps determine its approach to war. But the deepest strand of Rawls' argument here involves the institutions that protect the freedom and equality of the citizenry. It is the institutions of a democracy that make the defense of democracy so important to its people. More precisely, it is the belief in the freedom and equality of one's own society—and the freedom and equality of the other societies of the world—that ultimately establishes the sense of a just and unjust war in a liberal regime.

Interpreted in this manner, it is the widespread belief *in reciprocity* that anchors the foreign policy of the ideal society. As the philosopher David

A. Reidy puts it "Reciprocity is, for Rawls and Rawlsian liberals, a root moral norm."[24] And this feature of Rawls' thought helps explain what otherwise might seem out of place. Rawls mentions universal health care, equal opportunities in education, full employment, religious toleration, and other factors—including the public funding of elections—*within* his chapter on democratic peace and his reply to political realism.[25] There is a connection between these institutions and the unwillingness of the ideal democracy to invade its neighbor. But Rawls' point here is not something like "going to school prevents war." The point involves the political culture these institutions help to create. The institutions of democracy turn freedom and equality and reciprocity into living ideals. They help promote the happiness of the people.[26]

### Political Taxonomy

Rawls believes the ideal democracy possesses a range of stabilizing features. In the ideal democracy, there is no such thing as a "belligerent public"—where the people pressure heads of state into an unjust war.[27] But the last feature of *The Law of Peoples* I would like to discuss in this context is Rawls' political taxonomy. Rawls speaks about *five* different kinds of regime in *The Law of Peoples,* not just two. He identifies a burdened society and a benevolent absolutism and a decent hierarchical society—as well as an outlaw regime and an ideal, democratic, liberal people. What role do these other types of regimes play in Rawls' argument?

As noted before, the goal of *The Law of Peoples* is to create a stable international system. The way societies *interact* with each other is Rawls' main concern. And this leads Rawls to develop a more detailed picture of the behavior of different societies in the international system. The empirical dimension of *The Law of Peoples* is far more pronounced than in earlier works.[28]

A more detailed picture of the international system is essential to Rawls' project in this book. The diversities of political life are directly engaged in *The Law of Peoples.* This does not mean, however, that the basic contention in Rawls' argument suddenly disappears. A key factor in Rawls' taxonomy involves the willingness of a state to wage an unjust war. Only the outlaw regime denies basic human rights *and* plans to go to war with its neighbors. None of the other regimes in Rawls' taxonomy possesses both of these features.

From this point of view, a decent hierarchical society and a benevolent absolutism are fundamentally different from the outlaw regime. These societies have achieved a lasting kind of stability in their internal organization and their foreign policy.[29] They will not destabilize the international system. And for Rawls, this is critical. A benevolent absolutism and a decent hierarchical society do not wage war to expand their power. Nor do these regimes systematically violate the basic human rights of their members. A concern for the lives of civilians is expressed. So, while it is true these regimes do not acknowledge the individual person in the manner of a liberal society, this does not mean these regimes are on par with Hitler's Germany. Decency and benevolence are also moral standards to Rawls—even though these standards lack the concern for freedom and equality reciprocity entails.

Interpreted in this manner, Rawls is accepting of a wide range of peaceful societies in *The Law of Peoples*. "Justice" and "liberal" are not synonyms in this text. But I think the real contrast here is not between the earlier and the later Rawls. The real contrast here lies with political realism. Rawls examines a range of characteristics in his political taxonomy. He looks at a society's institutions and legal system as well as its foreign policy and political culture. It is a very broad assessment that Rawls presents.[30] A political realist, however, has a highly reductive view of political life. Military strength and military weakness are the defining categories for a political realist. And the starkest expression of this difference involves the way Rawls and a political realist view a burdened society. In Rawls' description, a burdened society lacks an effective government and suffers from wide swaths of extreme poverty. The economic and political institutions of a burdened society are not well developed. But instead of seeing a burdened society as an opportunity for expansion—as the political realist does—Rawls response to a burdened society is to offer assistance. Rawls believes the ideal democracy must provide foreign aid to this people.[31]

From this point of view, Rawls responds to the perception of military weakness in a fundamentally different way than the political realist. There are few divides in political life as large as this.

### A Common Thread

The preceding comments have tried to speak to what is new in *The Law of Peoples*. Rawls offers a more detailed assessment of an outlaw regime in this book. He analyzes the period leading up to the Second World War in terms of an international system of highly unequal states. He believes the internal structure of the ideal democracy makes it less likely to pursue unjust wars. And he offers a more detailed picture of the international system. But to me, the most noteworthy difference between *The Law of Peoples* and *A Theory of Justice* is Rawls' inclusion of the duty of assistance within this work. In particular, section 57 and 58 of *A Theory of Justice* make no mention of foreign aid.

From all of these points of view—and others that I have not addressed—*The Law of Peoples* adds novel features to Rawls' foreign policy. But in assessing these new aspects of *The Law of Peoples* it is important to remember Rawls' ultimate goal. Rawls sets up *The Law of Peoples* as a response to political realism. The critique of political realism is the common thread that unites all of Rawls' foreign policy discussions. In my view, the arguments within *The Law of Peoples* are best understood in terms of this critique. This is the perspective I will adopt as the commentary proceeds.

## NOTES

1. Rawls believes the simultaneous pursuit of colonies by England, France and Germany—within a more general context of state rivalry—ultimately caused World War I. See *The Law of Peoples*, 53-54.

2. Rawls, *The Laws of Peoples*, 37. These rules are the substance of the international social contract

3. Rawls, *A Theory of Justice*, 324.

4. Ibid., 333.

5. Ibid., 334.

6. Ibid., 334.

7. Ibid., 334.

8. Ibid., 335.

9. Ibid., 335

10. Ibid., 331.

11. Ibid., 332.

12. Ibid., 325.

13. Ibid,. 332.

14. See the chapter on "Political Economy" below.

15. Stein, *Nuclear Weapons and Christian Conscience*, 29.

16. Rawls does not frame Truman's rationale in quite this manner. Instead, Rawls highlights Truman's desire to save the lives of American soldiers that might have been lost in an eventual invasion of Japan. See *The Law of Peoples*, 100.

17. Ibid., 95.

18. The passage from *A Theory of Justice* p. 325 cited earlier also uses this phrase.

19. Rawls, *The Law of Peoples*, 8, 54.

20. Ibid., 8, 54. Note how Rawls describes the *ideal* democracy as the antithesis of the outlaw regimes of the early modern period in both of these passages.

21. Rawls, *A Theory of Justice*, 334.

22. An early version of this argument is present—in very abstract form—in *A Theory of Justice*: "Indeed, civil disobedience (and conscientious refusal as well) is one of the stabilizing devices of a constitutional system. . . . Along with such things as free and regular elections and an independent judiciary empowered to interpret the constitution (not necessarily written), civil disobedience used with due restraint and sound judgment helps to maintain and strengthen just institutions. By resisting injustice within the limits of fidelity to the law, it serves to inhibit departures from injustice and to correct them when they occur." (Ibid., 336.)

23. Rawls cites Kant's notion of a *foedus pacificum*—a peaceful federation of societies—in this context. This idea, however, was not limited to Kant. Bentham, Thomas Paine and others made similar arguments. See Levy and Thompson, *Causes of War*, 83—as well as 69, 104 and 109.

24. Martin and Reidy, *Rawls's Law of Peoples: A Realistic Utopia?*, 177.

25. Rawls, *The Law of Peoples*, 50. Interpreting the claims made on this page—*in terms of Rawls' response to political realism*—will take up the bulk of the discussion in the next four chapters.

26. Ibid., 46-48.

27. Levy and Thompson, *Causes of War*, 110-111. The authors cite the Spanish-American War of 1898 as an example of a belligerent public. They also cite Kennedy's unwillingness to withdraw from the Vietnam War before the election of 1964 in this context. In particular, the authors believed Kennedy was unwilling to exit the war "because he feared that he would be blamed politically for losing Vietnam to the communists."

28. There are many examples of this in *The Law of Peoples*. The tendency of democracies to avoid wars with each other has already been identified in the introduction. However, Rawls' claims about the empirical causes of population growth are also critically important to the overall argument. See the chapter on primary schools below.

29. Rawls, *The Laws of Peoples*, 92.

30. Ibid., 64-65

31. Ibid., 37-38.

# TWO

## Elections

In the preceding chapter, I traced the development of Rawls' foreign policy from *A Theory of Justice* to *The Law of Peoples*. And while the two texts are not identical in all respects they share many of the same arguments and assumptions. In particular, Rawls' critique of political realism is a defining feature of both his early and his later work.

The comments made in the previous chapter have affected the way I will develop Rawls' argument. Instead of offering a lengthy interpretation of a decent hierarchical society I will focus on the ideal democracy presented in section 5 of *The Law of Peoples*. Rawls' reply to political realism is the dominant theme of this section and has implications for all of the regimes described in Rawls' international system. Diminishing extreme inequality—in every society—is a core goal of *The Law of Peoples*.

### 1. THE ARMED FORCES

I would like to begin this discussion of extreme inequality by further characterizing the domestic policy of a political realist. In particular, I would like to ask the question: what does the political relation look like to a thinker who does *not* affirm the right to vote? What is the status of heads of state and the armed forces—in a highly stratified early modern European regime?

Consider, in this context, Machiavelli's book *The Prince*. In this text—first made public in 1532—Machiavelli claims the following: "there is no proportion between one who is armed and one who is unarmed, and it is

not reasonable that whoever is armed obey willingly whoever is unarmed, and that someone unarmed be secure among armed servants."[1]

In this passage, a basic assumption of Machiavelli's thought is exposed. When it comes to the use of force, Machiavelli does not speak
about the freedom and equality of the person. Instead, Machiavelli believes the willingness to use weapons of war creates a basic division in
society. A society must always be understood in terms of those who can
fight and those who cannot.

Machiavelli's claim here is both exceedingly simple and very extreme.
The difference between an unarmed child and an armed soldier is so
large as to be a difference in kind. A child does not yet possess the power
of life and death. And if one thinks of the commander of an army, this
difference in power is magnified many times over. The commander of an
army wields the power of life and death on the largest of scales. There is
no "proportion" between the commander of an army and a child—or
unarmed person.

### The Political Relation

Machiavelli sees the power of the army in terms of the hierarchy it
creates: an army establishes a basic division in any society. As a consequence, Machiavelli has a very different view of the political relation than
has been discussed so far. The role of the person and the army in Machiavelli's thought is not the same as the role of the person and the army in
*The Law of Peoples*.

This point can be put another way. The political relation defines the
relationship between civilians, heads of state and the armed forces in a
society. It speaks to the status of different groups within society—relative
to each other. But there is more than one way to order this relation. The
political relation can be described in different terms.

For Rawls, the political relation is described in terms of the civilian
population. Government exists to protect the rights of civilians. The powers of government affirm the individual person. Machiavelli, however, is
focused on the role of the armed forces in a state: in Machiavelli's view,
whoever commands the armed forces of a society has the power to rule.
As a consequence, the civilian population does not center the regime in
Machiavelli's picture. Government does not exist to protect the rights of
the person. Instead, the civilian population is at the mercy of whoever

commands the armed forces. Whoever gives orders to the army can order the people.

Understood in this way, it is not an accident that Machiavelli speaks of "the prince" whereas Rawls speaks of "peoples." The prince is the person who commands an army and thus orders society. Machiavelli's picture of political life discounts civilians.

## The Great and the People

Machiavelli thinks of the political relation in hierarchical terms. There is no proportion between the civilian population and the commander of an army. And by the civilian population Machiavelli probably means all parts of society not devoted to war. Infants, children, those who are elderly, those who are ill—in short, anyone who does not wield a weapon—are at the mercy of those who do wield a weapon. In Machiavelli's picture, being unarmed is a failing.

From the point of view of contemporary human rights doctrine, using weapons of war against unarmed civilians is both immoral and illegal. It is a war crime or a crime against humanity and is unambiguously condemned.[2] Machiavelli, however, does not think like this at all. Instead, Machiavelli is obsessed with commanding an army. The prince must gain the loyalty of an army to counteract the army of his competitors. A prince without an army cannot succeed.

Machiavelli's understanding of the political relation gives *The Prince* its militaristic tone. The ideals of *individual* freedom and equality—and the practices informed by these ideals—are not major parts of Machiavelli's thought. Machiavelli's hierarchical understanding of political life, however, is not limited to the prince and his army. Machiavelli also divides society up between "the great" and "the people." There is a small upper class and a large under-class in *The Prince*.

This point can be put another way. In Machiavelli's text, all members of society do not have the same power or status. Not every person can command an army. This asymmetry, however, is evident in other areas of life. The individuals with the most resources and influence in a society have a special political rank. Members of the great are able to act politically.

Understood in this way, the great are the individuals who possess more wealth, or have sway among the ranks of the armed forces, or retain some other special status or privilege. The great are individuals who have been favored by "Fortune." The people, on the other hand, are individuals who—for whatever reason—cannot take part in the competition for power. The people do not have large amounts of resources and are not in a position to command an army. Fortune has not favored the people in the same way.

Seen in this light, there are several types of inequality in Machiavelli's thought. There is the difference in power between those who are armed and those who are not. There are also differences in power between the great and the people. In these and other ways, a Machiavellian society is highly unequal.

*Civil War*

As can be seen from this brief summary, Machiavelli thinks about the political relation in very different terms from Rawls. Machiavelli speaks at length about princes and the great and armies and fortune. But he spends almost no time at all speaking of the people and their needs.[3] Meeting the urgent needs of the people is not the defining task of the prince.

The hierarchical quality of Machiavelli's thought is very extreme. In this respect, *The Prince* mirrors the extreme inequality that pervaded Europe throughout the early modern period. However—and perhaps surprisingly—Machiavelli does speak about elections in *The Prince*. What does he have to say about this institution?

The key point here is a point about strength. In a deeply divided society that lacks elections, regime change is very often violent. The person seeking power must raise an army of his own to counteract the army of the existing ruler. But in a regime with elections the situation is different. The division of society into armed factions is less likely to occur.

Consider, in this context, Machiavelli's description of the Ottoman Empire. In Machiavelli's narrative, the Ottoman Empire was not a hereditary monarchy: "For it is not the sons of the old prince who are the heirs and become the lords, but the one who is elected to that rank by those who have the authority for it."[4] The ruler of the Ottoman Empire did not inherit the throne. Command of the armed forces was transferred through an election. On the other hand, Machiavelli is clearly not talking about universal suffrage in this passage. Instead, his picture involves a certain class of people—"those who have authority"—selecting a ruler. The ability to vote is restricted to a small number of persons.

In the passage on the Ottoman Empire, Machiavelli is not operating with the principle "one person, one vote." Elections are the provenance of the great, not the people. Elections in the Ottoman Empire, however, do have their benefits:

> And this being an ancient order (e.g. the holding of regular elections), one cannot call it a new principality, because some of the difficulties of new principalities are not in it: for if the prince is indeed new, the orders of that state are old and are ordered to receive him as if he were their hereditary lord. [5]

The argument here is extremely important. Regimes with elections have a distinctive look. On one hand, elections break the grip of hereditary succession. Elections allow individuals to gain power who are not members of a royal family. From this point of view, elections allow a person who is "new" to rule. On the other hand, elections avoid "some of the difficulties" that arise from the overthrow of a regime.[6] In particular, the fragmentation of society into armed factions is not necessary in a regime with elections. Political transitions do not diminish the power of the state.

Understood in this way, a regime with elections is a kind of political hybrid. It retains the concept of loyalty but does not define loyalty in terms of allegiance to a person or family. Instead, the armed forces expect leaders who are new and different. New leaders are viewed "as if" they are "hereditary lords."

## 2. FALLIBILITY

Machiavelli understands elections in terms of the hereditary and hierarchical regimes of the early modern period. In a regime with elections, the power of the army is not divided against itself. But what does Rawls have to say about an election? How does Rawls view this institution?

Consider some of the features of what Rawls' calls an "established democracy" in *The Law of Peoples*. In an established democracy, elections are held at regular intervals. Elections usually occur every few years. And, while the speeches and policies of a head of state might prove persuasive in one election, this does not mean the speeches and policies of a head of state will always prove persuasive. An idea may not work out in the way envisioned. There might be very large unintended consequences associated with policy.

Understood in this way, elections introduce a sense of *fallibility* into democratic politics. New events—and the poor performance of ideas—can lead to very different political debates. Moreover, the introduction of fallibility into the political process has far reaching consequences in Rawls' view. No single election might achieve the public good. But the process of testing policies over time can move a society in the direction of the public good. Individual moments in the process are fallible. The process as a whole, however, might display improvement.

The political culture of an established democracy is built on notions of fallibility—and progress. The erroneous policies of the past can be adjusted. A second point: in an established democracy, elections do not immediately solve all political problems. It is a mistake to assume the same set of policies will always work. But what elections do accomplish is the insertion of the needs of the people into the political process. Heads of state cannot wield power if they do not persuade a majority—or a plurality—of the people who vote that their policies are better than the policies of a competitor. Heads of state must win over the belief of the people every few years.

Interpreted in this manner, there are two features that characterize the political culture of an established democracy. The first is an assumption that policy is fallible and can be adjusted over time. The second assumption involves the role of the people in determining the success or failure of a policy. In an established democracy, the civilian population ultimately steers the regime.

*Two Images of Politics*

In Rawls' interpretation, elections do not enhance the power of the already powerful. Elections are not focused on the needs of "the great."[7] Instead, elections allow the question "Are the people happy?" to be asked anew. The happiness of the people is Rawls' focus. But the final comment I would like to make in this context involves the *expectations* of work in an established democracy. In a democracy, hope—the felt belief in progress—is a political emotion.

Rawls draws out this aspect of democratic political culture in a passage on St. Just:

> As Saint Just said, 'The idea of happiness is new in Europe.' What he
> meant was that *the social order was no longer viewed as fixed: political and*

*social institutions could be revised and reformed for the purpose of making
peoples happier and more satisfied. (italics mine)*[8]

The claim here is striking. The image of politics as progressive—promoting the happiness of the people—is antithetical to the image of politics as static, with the place of one's birth determining one's chance of success. In a functioning democracy, children tend to have more opportunities than their parents. Notice, however, that Rawls' claim here is framed in terms of the mental life of civilians. The way people "view" or percieve political life has undergone a transformation. The citizens in a democracy anticipate improvement in their children's lives.

Or, to put this point another way: in the early modern period of Europe, the image of society was both unchanging and hierarchical. In this context, a picture of the social order as fixed sees the distinction between peasants and aristocrats, subjects and kings, colonized peoples and empire, as existing indefinitely into the future. The social order as it is will exist in perpetuity. And the fact that one has no control over the place of one's birth—the fact that no child decides to be born a peasant or a slave or the eldest son in a royal family—is simply not relevant in this picture. Political life cannot change one's destiny or fate.

Interpreted in this manner, the early modern state in Europe had a tragic description of the people and their needs. The suffering of the people is not something political life can change or address. But in Rawls' view, the shift to democracy fundamentally alters the picture. The removal of suffering becomes a political goal.

### A Little Better

In Rawls' view, the surfacing of democracy—out of a continent dominated by princes and kings—is a tectonic shift in political life. Instead of a hierarchical image of society, forever ruled by royal families, society is now understood as changing and evolving in accordance with the needs of the people. The social order is tested and possibly reformed with each election cycle.

The view of social and political institutions as open to change is a core notion of *The Law of Peoples*. Indeed, the hope and optimism of this text— the belief that political injustice can be slowly removed from the earth— has its roots in this discussion.[9] If one does not believe the basic institutions of society can be changed and adjusted to better meet the needs of the people, little of Rawls' political philosophy will prove persuasive.

Rawls believes political institutions can be improved with time and experience. A society can learn from the mistakes of the past. But this claim must not be understood as a claim about perfection. Rawls' language here is the language of the editor. "Revised" and "reformed" are the terms invoked.

From this point of view, Rawls' political philosophy is one of perfectibility—not perfection. Rawls' political philosophy is the philosophy of "a little better." And this is very important for understanding the tone of *The Law of Peoples*. The earliest regimes with elections in Europe were shot through with injustice. They were hierarchical and expansionist in ways that Rawls clearly condemns. But at least a regime with free elections and public debate sets in motion a process that allows for change and improvement. In a regime with elections, citizens at least come to expect what is new and different.

## A Contrast

In this chapter, I have highlighted two alternative ways of characterizing an election. Machiavelli is concerned with the way elections enhance the military power of the state. Elections transfer power without dividing the army. Rawls, however, emphasizes the notion of progress in his account of elections. The holding of regular elections make possible gradual change and improvement in the lives of civilians. In point of fact, Rawls believes the existence of armies in a society is only made necessary by the existence of outlaw regimes. If there were no dangerous hostile states, a police force alone would suffice.[10] This in itself shows how far Rawls is from Machiavelli's perspective. The responsiveness of representatives to the needs of the people—not the expansion of the head of state's military power—is the decisive feature of an election for Rawls.[11]

## NOTES

1. Machiavelli, *The Prince*, 58.
2. Stephen Nathanson's *Terrorism and the Ethics of War* draws attention to the Protocols of the 1977 additions to the Geneva Conventions. In particular Protocol I, chapter II, article 51. 2. states that: "The civilian population as such, as well as individual civilians, shall not be the object of attack. Acts or threats of violence the primary purpose of which is to spread terror among the civilian population are prohibited."

Nathanson claims the purpose of his text is to "solidify the standing of these firm principals within a rule-utilitarian perspective." Nathanson, *Terrorism and the Ethics of War*, 213.

3. In chapter 9 of *The Prince*, Machiavelli claims the people desire "to not be commanded or oppressed by the great." In the last chapter of *The Prince*, entitled "Exhortation to Seize Italy and to Free Her from the Barbarians," Machiavelli outlines the desire of the Italians to fend off invasion. In the first case, freedom is freedom from domestic powers. In the second case, freedom is freedom from foreign powers. Machiavelli, *The Prince*, 39, 101-105. From this point of view, Machiavelli's thought is moving towards the interpretation of *freedom* described by Locke.

4. Ibid., 82.

5. Ibid., 82.

6. In chapter 3 of *The Prince* Machiavelli claims that: "... one must always offend those over whom he becomes a new prince, both with men-at-arms and with infinite other injuries." As a consequence, the new leader has "as enemies all those whom he offended in seizing the principality." Ibid., 8.

7. Rawls' insistence on the public funding is grounded in this point. In the absence of this institution, existing concentrations of wealth and power can capture the political process, ultimately affecting the kinds of candidates that can successfully compete for office. See Rawls, *The Law of Peoples*, 50.

8. Rawls, *The Law of Peoples*, 46.

9. Ibid., p. 6-7.

10. See Rawls, *The Law of Peoples*, 26.

11. In Rawls' account, a benevolent absolutism lacks elections altogether while a decent hierarchical society does not affirm each person's right to vote. And yet, Rawls believes these societies are minimally just. How does all of this fit together with this account of elections? I think the key issue for Rawls in this context is the *responsiveness* of the government to the needs of the people. For instance, Rawls claims that all regimes must take measures to prevent famines. A state that allows its people to starve to death is radically unjust. (Ibid., 109) More generally, *decency* and *benevolence* are moral standards to Rawls They are attitudes that rule out cruelty and neglect—even though decency and benevolence do not contain specific concerns for freedom and equality that reciprocity entails. For more on the theme of preventing famines in *The Law of Peoples*, see chapter 5.

# THREE

## Public Health

Elections promote the happiness of the people. In a democracy the removal of unnecessary suffering from society is a political goal. This account of liberal democracy, however, is very abstract. Elections make heads of state responsive to the needs of the people. But what specific policies must a democracy adopt in Rawls' view? And how can these policies be amended — to better meet the needs of the people?

In this chapter, I respond to these questions by focusing on the theme of health care in a democracy. In Rawls' view, a society cannot provide basic health care to some persons while denying basic health care to their peers. Instead, a liberal democracy must assure "basic health care for all."[1] Each person has a right to basic care.

Moreover, in reflecting on the importance of public health, a few of Rawls' underlying assumptions about society will come out into the open. In particular, Rawls believes a society must be understood as persisting through time. The needs of a society include the needs of a society's future members.[2]

As a consequence, Rawls places a great deal of weight on intergenerational questions in his political philosophy. A society must be organized in such a way that its principles and institutions are affirmed — and improved — over time as new generations of citizens are born and develop. If a society fails to renew its principles and institutions over time, extreme inequalities will appear again. A highly stratified class structure will re-emerge.

## 1. WASHING CHILDREN

Rawls believes health care is a right in a liberal democracy. No citizen can be denied basic care. But what were some of the first expressions of public health as a concept—in the early modern period in Europe? How did the ideal of public health get off the ground—in the social contract tradition?

Consider the following statement about the health of children in Locke's *A Letter Concerning Toleration*: "if the Magistrate understands washing to be profitable to the curing of any Disease that children are subject unto, and esteem the matter weighty enough that it can be taken care of by a Law, in that case he may order it to be done."[3]

In this passage, childhood disease comes to light as negative or bad. It is not a good thing for society to have sick and dying children. However, what is distinctive about this passage in *A Letter Concerning Toleration* is not the claim that disease is bad. Anyone who has been ill can vouch for this fact. What is distinctive about this passage is the way Locke describes childhood disease as a concern of government. The "Magistrate"—i.e., *parliament*—can improve childhood health.

From this point of view, the passage on washing children is making two kinds of claims. The first claim is a negative statement about disease. There is something obviously harmful about disease and illness. Disease and illness can have substantial impacts on society as a whole. The second claim is a positive statement about government. The elected officials of a country can do something about disease and illness. Representatives can pass laws that promote the health of children.

### The Health of Adults

Locke believes the practice of washing children benefits the child. Washing a child increases the chance of that child's survival. Still, one might be wondering: why not help adults as well as children? Why not protect all citizens from disease?[4]

This point can be put another way. Children are the future labor and work and "strength" of society. Today's children are tomorrow's parents. As a consequence, a law promoting the health of children benefits society as a whole. The public good is advanced through this act of parliament. And yet, as important as washing is, a law mandating the washing of children is clearly not enough to guarantee childhood health. The health of children depends on many factors—including the health of adults. Infants are directly threatened by the death of their parents.

From this point of view, Locke's approach to public health is not as effective as it could be. Healthy parents are needed to improve the health of children. The model of childhood health in Locke's law is *incomplete*.

Locke's law about the washing of children is insufficient to achieve the goals Locke himself established as valid. Bathing a child is clearly not enough to ensure that child's survival. A second criticism of Locke's argument, however—and this criticism gets to the heart of the matter—is that it is *inhumane*. Adults are also persons who are vulnerable to disease and can suffer terribly. Why be so unresponsive to the health of adults?

The urgency of this question is obvious enough when thinking about the plague that struck London in 1665 during Locke's life. It is estimated than one in six persons living in London died from this outbreak of infectious disease in a single year.[5] But consider also the influenza epidemic of 1918. In this pandemic, fifty million people died around the world, with some estimates ranging as high as one-hundred million persons. That is to say, roughly three percent *of the world's population* died from the H1N1 virus in this period.[6]

The influenza epidemic of 1918 might be the largest epidemic to ever affect the human species.[7] Several hundred million persons became ill with influenza in a two-year period. And one might assume that children were the primary victims of this outbreak of influenza: in subsequent influenza outbreaks, children have clearly been at very high risk. The victims of the H1N1 virus of 1918, however, were predominantly young adults. Individuals between the ages of eighteen and thirty-five died in the greatest numbers.[8]

Understood in this way, the argument that infants and children—but not adults—should be protected from influenza makes zero sense. Leaving the adult population out of the government response to influenza would be a terrible mistake. What is more, the global outbreak of a new variant of the H1N1 virus—in 2009—was met with a massive distribution of vaccine to both children and adults in many countries around the world. The argument "Only children should receive the vaccine" was not heard.[9]

## 2. EXTREME INEQUALITY

Locke's law about washing children amounts to a first stab at public health, not a working definition. Nevertheless a crucial point about public health has come to light. When it comes to public health, the unit of analysis must be all persons. Excluding individuals or groups of people from basic health care is both ineffective and needlessly cruel.

Reflecting on Locke's mandate to wash the children is a start. But what of Rawls' account of health care in *The Law of Peoples*? How does Rawls' frame a society's commitment to public health?

The key difference between Rawls and Locke is Rawls' insistence that health care is an individual right, whereas Locke understands the health of children as a "public good."[10] In Rawls' view, every citizen—both child and adult—must have access to basic care.

Or, to speak more precisely: there are three very general types of justification for public health in the social contract tradition. One form of justification focuses on the public good of the nation. The way a health law contributes to *the strength* of society is that law's ultimate justification. This is the approach taken by Locke in *A Letter Concerning Toleration*.

A second approach to public health is defended in John Stuart Mill's *Utilitarianism*. In this text, disease is a major cause of suffering in society. Disease can cause intense pain or chronic pain—or both. But for Mill, there is nothing inevitable about the suffering caused by disease. Outbreaks of diseases like the plague are not destined to be a permanent part of the human condition. Just the opposite: scientific "progress" coupled with control of "noxious influences" and better "education" holds out hope for a future free from this "detestable foe."[11] Social policy can minimize and ultimately remove this cause of human suffering.

Locke believed caring for children would promote the strength of society while Mill offered a humanitarian defense of public health. The approach Rawls takes toward public health, however, is broader than the approach taken by Locke and Mill. That is to say: assuring health care for every person is useful to society. It benefits all citizens, both present and future. Universal care, however, also prevents "extreme forms of inequality" from taking root in society.[12] The ideal of equality is at stake in Rawls' account.

*A Comparison*

In Rawls' view, the *political* status of citizens—relative to each other—is at issue in a society's health care policies. Health care affects *the political relation*. But why does Rawls make this claim about health care? Why connect the absence of health care with extreme inequality?

One way to understand Rawls' argument here is to think in terms of a societal comparison. What differences arise between persons who receive basic health care and persons who do not receive basic health care in a society? How do individuals who receive basic health care fare—relative to those who do not?

From Rawls' point of view, the answer to this question is not mysterious or hard to fathom. It is quite clear. A society that does not assure health care for every person—a society where, for instance, some children receive basic health care but other children do not—has created a very deep division. These two groups of children do not begin life in the same place.

In particular, an infant with access to basic health care is aided by several centuries of medical science. Insights into the causes of illness and disease—as well as insights into their prevention and treatment—can be used by doctors to help this person. On the other hand, infants who do not have access to basic health care lack this kind of aid. All of the hard won insights into the causes and treatments of disease—the several-hundred-year development of medical science—do not touch the infant's life. The initial gift the child receives from the adult world is not the same.

*Effects*

A society that does not assure basic health care to all children has created fundamentally different starting points in the life of its citizens. And this is true no matter how loving a family one is born into. A child with access to basic health care begins life with a very big boost.

Nor should this claim be understood in abstract terms. Medical interventions in the life of children can make a huge difference. A child with an untreated illness—a child with an infection who does not have access to basic health care—can encounter all kinds of difficulties related to this illness for the rest of her life. That is to say: a child is 1) more likely to live, and 2) more likely to live free of disease *if* they have access to basic care.

To speak again to an extreme example: the effects of malaria on the life of a child are very acute and can be lethal; according to the World Health Organization, "young children contribute the bulk of malaria deaths worldwide."[13] And even if the child is able to live with this parasite, her ability to develop and give back to society in the future can be greatly diminished. Preventing infection—and treating infection if prevention fails—makes a massive difference, both in terms of the suffering of the child and her future contributions.

A child infected with malaria will not be able to function at the same level as a healthy peer. The starting points of children with malaria and children without malaria are radically different. And what is true of young malaria victims is true of adult malaria victims. Adults with untreated malaria infections are not in the same position as their treated peers.[14] They suffer more—and their ability to make contributions to society is greatly reduced.[15]

## Basic Care

Rawls defends health care in political terms. The equal status of the person in society is threatened by disease. The final comment I would like to make about health care in this context concerns Rawls use of the word "basic" in the principle "basic health care for all." What exactly does Rawls mean by this term?

Rawls does not specify the content of basic care. And there are political reasons for this. Basic care can differ somewhat between democracies—the elected representatives of disparate peoples might choose to prioritize different kinds of care.[16] But a second reason for reticence here might be the nature of medical research and practice. Medical research has not reached a comfortable resting place when it comes to disease and illness. There is still an overwhelming amount of work to do.

Or, to put this point in different terms: the concept of a virus and a parasite and bacteria did not exist in the seventeenth century.[17] The microscope had just been introduced into England during Locke's life. But why would one argue that the late seventeenth century picture of disease should establish the meaning of basic care for all future persons? Who would want to be treated *now* with *Locke's* concept of disease? But just as it is possible to criticize Locke's model of disease from the perspective of contemporary medical practice, so will it be possible, in the future, to look back at the medical knowledge and practices of 2012 and say: "This was not so good."

From this point of view, fixing health care to some standard in the past is a mistake. Nor is resting content with current medical practice the best of all possible options. Instead, a commitment to universal health care requires a lasting commitment to the institutions that make health care possible (a medical system) and allow it to improve (a system of scientific research). In this way, the health care needs of all persons in society can be better met.

## *Progress*

In this chapter, Rawls account of public health has been described in greater detail. In Rawls' view, a society cannot provide basic care to some persons while denying basic care to their neighbors. A fair society must provide basic care to all persons. Every person has a right to basic care. And, while Rawls does not make this explicit in the text, one can imagine a connection between the holding of regular elections—described in the last chapter—and the provision of health care. In particular, a society where each citizen has the right to vote insures the public health of society remains an issue in every election. The health care policies of the society can be continually remade as the needs and understanding of the public shifts.[18]

## NOTES

1. Rawls, *The Law of Peoples*, 50.
2. Renewing society requires the *simultaneous* affirmation of several distinct but essential standards: "Among these values are the equality of women, the equality of children as the future citizens, and finally, the value of the family in securing the orderly production and reproduction of society and of its culture from one generation to the next . . ." Rawls, *Justice as Fairness: A Restatement*, 168.
3. Locke, *A Letter Concerning Toleration*, 32.
4. The error here is in Locke's model of adult illness. Negligence is not the only cause—or the main cause, or even a minor cause—of adult illness.
5. See the entry "The Great Plague of London 1665-1666" in The National Archives (United Kingdom): www.nationalarchives.gov.uk/education/lesson49.htm
6. Taubenberger, Jeffrey K.; Morens, David M. "1918 Influenza: the Mother of All Pandemics." www.ncbi.nlm.nih.gov/pmc/articles/PMC3291398/
7. Ibid.
8. Ibid.

9. In personal correspondence, Dr. Yonatan Grad makes the following observation about the distribution of vaccine: "While generally, yes, public health authorities try to protect the entire public, there are some subtleties to this. If, for whatever reason, access to vaccine was limited, you'd have to make a choice about who should receive vaccine. When the swine flu H1N1 vaccine became available in limited quantities, people made judgments about which populations to vaccinate first, and chose those at highest risk for severe disease (e.g. pregnant women, the immuno-compromised). Also, children seem to be predominant vectors for influenza, and vaccinating them may protect the entire community to a significant degree." For more on the effects of vaccinating children against influenza see the article "Effect of Influenza Vaccination of Children on Infection Rates in Hutterite Communities: A Randomized Trial" published in the *Journal of the American Medical Association*. http://jama.jamanetwork.com/article.aspx?articleid=185509

10. Locke invokes "the public good" to justify new positive laws in *A Letter Concerning Toleration*: "The Public Good is the Rule and Measure of All Lawmaking. If a thing is not useful to the commonwealth . . . it cannot be established by Law." Locke, *A Letter Concerning Toleration*, 39. From this point of view, the public good—as discerned by the (male) civilian population and (male) elected representatives—can build upon the framework of law mandated by the "natural rights" of the (male) person.

11. John Stuart Mill, *Utilitarianism*, 14-15.

12. Rawls, *The Law of Peoples*, 53.

13. World Health Organization Malaria Fact Sheet April 2010. For more recent numbers see: www.who.int/world_malaria_report_2011_factsheet.pdf

14. The World Health Organization reports 247 million cases of malaria worldwide and 1 million fatalities in 2008.

15. The WHO estimates that "Malaria can decrease gross domestic product by as much as 1.3 percent in countries with high disease rates."

16. For more on this topic, see chapter 8.

17. The germ theory of disease came about in the nineteenth century. Viruses were not identified until the twentieth century.

18. Rawls does not make the same claim about disease as he makes about famine in *The Law of Peoples*. In particular, Rawls does not claim that all societies must protect all civilians from disease. It is difficult, however, to interpret the significance of this omission. As David A. Reidy notes "Rawls clearly thinks that the suffering of individual persons in burdened societies is fundamental to the justification of the duty of assistance, a duty which effectively makes basic human rights a foreign policy imperative for all states." (Reidy and Martin, *Rawls's Law of Peoples, A Realistic Utopia?*, 175) So, while Rawls does not explicitly identify Article 25 of The Universal Declaration of Human Rights—which names a right to health care—among his list of *basic* human rights this does not mean he is unconcerned about health care in other societies. Cholera, malaria, influenza, HIV/AIDS, tuberculosis and other forms of diseases clearly cause suffering and lead to death. A decent hierarchical society and a benevolent absolutism must, I think, be concerned with the health of the civilian population in some minimal way. For Rawls' treatment of this theme in the context of the duty of assistance, see *The Law of Peoples*, 114.

# FOUR

# Primary Schools

A society in which some receive health care while others do not is highly unequal: all persons in a liberal society must have access to medical care. It is important, however, to avoid interpreting the causes of inequality in too narrow a fashion. Disease is not the only cause of extreme inequality.

In particular, Rawls believes a society where some children attend primary school while others do not is deeply divided. Failing to train the mental abilities of all persons is a cause of extreme inequality.[1] Similarly, a society in which some are employed while others are not employed is deeply divided. Unemployment—like the lack of a primary school education—leads to class formation. Rawls also finds a source of extreme inequality in the way elections are funded. Without the "public funding of elections," a democracy is in danger of becoming a democracy in name but an oligarchy in fact.[2] Extreme concentrations of wealth can easily capture the election process.

Seen in this light, Rawls does not mention one single cause of inequality in *The Law of Peoples*. He mentions several predictable causes of extreme inequality. He has a model of extreme inequality in section 5 of this text.

## 1. THE MENTAL LIFE OF CHILDREN

Rawls believes a fair medical system makes a society less divided over time. Infectious disease need not lead to an underclass. But why are primary schools a condition of equality? Why train the mental abilities of all citizens?

Here again it might help to reframe this question in terms of a comparison. Consider a society in which the mental abilities of boys are trained while the mental abilities of girls and women are neglected. What happens in this situation? What happens when only boys can attend primary school?

Again the answer here is not mysterious. It is quite obvious. In this kind of society, a very deep division is established. How will a child who cannot read and write and cannot perform more complicated operations in math and science fare as she grows older? What occupations will be open to her, as she becomes an adult?[3] More precisely, what occupations will be open to women if only male children have gone to school? How will labor and work be divided in a society with such unequal training?

Understood in this way, the educational practices of a society do not have a momentary or transitory impact on the lives of children. The educational practices of society have a lasting impact on the lives of children. The child who attends primary school is given a very large boost. There are more employment opportunities available to her.

### The Footrace

The comparison between a person whose abilities are trained in school and a person whose abilities are not trained in school is one way to explain the need for a universal system of primary schooling. Another intuitive way to understand this point is to consider an analogy. If one imagines a foot race—where many people are competing to cross the finish line ahead of their neighbors—it is very clear that a person who starts fifty yards behind her peers has little chance of winning. In this situation, the starting point in the foot race clearly affects the outcome the participants can achieve.

Similarly—"by analogy"—children who do not attend primary school are at a very great disadvantage relative to those who do. These two groups of children do not begin their lives in the same place. Moreover, this difference in starting points impacts the outcomes each group can achieve. The consequences of unequal education and training do not simply fade away over time.

The analogy between the footrace and primary schooling is just an analogy. And it is a mistake to describe the fundamental relations between the members of society entirely in terms of a competition. Still, the analogy does capture a powerful intuition about justice or fairness. A society is not fair if its children are allowed to begin life in such different conditions.

### Written Exchange

The analogy of the footrace draws attention to a facet of justice: the justice of a process depends, in part, on the initial conditions of that process. A competition is not fair if there is no chance of winning. But it may help to make this discussion of primary school training a little more concrete. What are some of the specific skills that are developed in primary school? And why are these skills so beneficial in a person's life?

Consider literacy in this context. Reading a language like English has several preconditions. A child must learn to speak English from other persons—a process which can begin even before the child is born.[4] A child must also make connections between an alphabet and the words she hears and speaks. Some understanding of syntax must develop.[5] And, as Rawls might say, "much, much else": learning to read is a complicated process. But at the end of this road all kinds of possibilities are opened up. I do not know how many books have been written in English. But there are many. And, in principle, I have access to every single one of these texts when I learn to read. The mental life of many other persons is available to me.

Interpreted in this manner, learning to read allows for new paths of communication and influence in the life of a person. A child will hear the words spoken to her and around her. But in addition to the persons heard in daily life, there are the written words the child can gain access to on the page. There is a new channel for language in the child's life. And this, to stress again, is not a minor point. It is very significant. A child who attends primary school and learns to read can tap into an immense repository of thought and reflection. Stories in English and stories translated into English, texts in math and science, the information contained in practical guides: all become possible experiences in the life of the reader. Nor should one forget about the internet in this context, which allows for written communication between persons across the globe. As the philosopher Kwame Anthony Appiah has noted, we can now "realistically imagine contacting" almost anyone on the earth.[6] The blending of experiences that goes on in written communication is really quite profound.

The child who is prevented from attending primary school, however, will have a much more difficult time gaining access to the written thoughts and ideas of other people. The child's capacity for independent action is also harmed.

*Self-Interpretation*

A lack of primary school education has a cascading effect on the mental life of the person. The individual is isolated from many parts of her culture when she cannot gain access to its written words. The effects of unequal primary schooling, however, are not limited to things like the ability to read. Unequal educational opportunities also play out on an interpersonal level. How will a sister view her own life if she is treated so differently from her brother? How does the preferential education of boys over girls affect a girl's self-interpretation?[7] This question must also be understood in the opposite direction. How will a brother understand the fact that his sister does not go to school? How does the preferential education of a boy over a girl in a family and society affect a boy's self-interpretation?

Infants and children cannot control the initial choices about how they are spoken to or what they can learn. The attitudes in a family and a society clearly matter here. Nor can one assume that these initial social interpretations quickly tail off once women grow older and new families are formed. How will men and women relate to each other if girls and women are denied primary schooling? How will a woman gain access to independent information—if no one helps her to read a book or a newspaper or other forms of the written word?

## 2. FEMALE LITERACY AND CHILDHOOD MORTALITY

Education and training affects a wide range of issues. A person's capacities, opportunities and self-interpretation are affected by primary schooling. But in order to better understand the empirical effects of education and training in the life of a people, it will help to consider the reflections on female education and literacy in the writings of Amartya Sen—an economist, Sanskritist, and colleague of Rawls who is cited at several key moments in *The Law of Peoples*.[8] How does Sen describe the effects of female literacy?

Sen—in his text *Development as Freedom*—notes that female literacy diminishes childhood mortality: "There is considerable evidence that women's education and literacy tend to reduce the mortality rates of children."[9] Fewer children die when women can read. Nor does Sen leave this point at a general level. A few pages on, he cites an empirical study to support this claim:

> Murthi, Guio, and Dreze's statistical analysis indicates that, in quantitative terms, the effect of female literacy on childhood mortality is extraordinarily large. It is a more powerful influence than the other variables that also work in this direction. For instance, keeping other variables constant, an increase in the crude female literacy rate from, say, 22 percent (the actual 1981 figure for India) to 75 percent reduces the predicted value of under-five mortality for males and females combined from 156 per thousand (again, the actual 1981 figure) to 110 per thousand.[10]

There are many points one can make here. Above all, it is important to remember the human dimension of these numbers. What does it mean for the individual women and men living in a society when the mental abilities of 78 percent of the female population have not been trained in school? What does it mean for individual children and parents when approximately 16 percent of all children die before they reach the age of 5? But this passage is not framed in terms of intractable problems that can never be solved. There is nothing fatalistic about Sen's writing. Instead, social policy can elevate the literacy of all children to the highest priority. Female literacy can most definitely be increased.[11] Moreover, increasing female literacy—which is a good in itself—also boosts the lives of children. In the study Sen references, female education reduces childhood mortality by almost 30 percent. The lives of many children have been saved by greater female literacy.

The study of Murthi, Guio and Dreze establishes an empirical basis for Sen's claims about female literacy. But if one asks the question "Why does female literacy reduce childhood mortality?" or "What lies behind these observations?" Sen offers an answer. Sen speaks at great lengths about the "agency effects" of female literacy. A women's capacity to influence decisions within the family and society is increased by primary schooling.

Or, to speak more precisely: Sen does not provide one single, definitive explanation of why schooling enhances female agency. Instead he
makes a number of different observations:

> There are, in fact, many different ways in which school education may
> enhance a young woman's decisional power within the family: through
> its effect on her social standing, her ability to be independent, her pow-
> er to articulate, her knowledge of the outside world, her skill in influ-
> encing group decisions and so on. [12]

In this passage, literacy and education affect the ability of women to get
things done within the family and within society. There is a link between
a woman's capabilities and her agency in society. But the picture here is
not one of a single skill saving the day. The picture is one of several skills
reinforcing each other. There are many effects associated with going to
school.

## 3. FEMALE LITERACY AND FERTILITY RATES

In Sen's view, increasing female literacy is a goal in its own right. Achiev-
ing literacy is an "end in itself" and must be given the highest priority.
Female literacy and education, however, are also a launching point for
many of the other specific claims Sen makes in this text—starting with
childhood health but also including other important goals. The effects of
female literacy are quite dramatic and run across a wide range of issues.

For instance, Sen notes that increasing literacy rates for women is
essential in reducing the fertility rate in a society:

> There is now quite extensive statistical evidence, based on comparison
> between different countries and different regions (that is, cross-section
> studies, as they are called), that link women's education (including
> literacy) and the lowering of fertility across different countries in the
> world. [13]

And when female education is combined with greater employment opportunities for women, the effects on fertility rates are even more profound: "In a comparative study of nearly three hundred districts within
India, it emerges that women's education and women's employment are
the two most important influences in reducing fertility rates." [14] In both of
these passages, the ability of young girls to go to school diminishes the
number of births in a country. But in a society with more employment

opportunities for women, these effects are even greater. The population of a society can begin to level off instead of exhibiting rapid growth.[15]

Sen's argument in this context is slightly different from his treatment of childhood mortality. Literacy and employment opportunities together can make the biggest difference. The basic point, however, is still one of agency. A woman who has gone to primary school and can work in environments outside of the home—a woman who has more of a say in the economic fortunes of the house and, Sen adds, greater control of her body through access to contraception—is involved in the decision to have children in new ways. The roles available to women in society also expand.

As was the case with his discussion of childhood mortality, Sen draws on the empirical study of Murthio, Guio and Dreze to make his point about fertility rates more concrete. He also draws on larger units of analysis. In regards to the Indian state of Kerala, Sen notes that the fertility rate fell from "forty four per one thousand in the 1950's to eighteen by 1991"—through improvements in female literacy, female employment and family planning.[16] Similarly, in Tamil Nadu, another state in India:

> Tamil Nadu, has had no slower a fall of fertility rate (than Kerala), from 3.5 in 1979 to 2.2 in 1991. Tamil Nadu has had an active, but cooperative, family planning program, and it could use for this purpose a comparatively good position in terms of social achievements in India: one of the highest literacy rates among the major Indian states, high female participation in gainful employment, and relatively low infant mortality.[17]

The reductions in fertility rates Sen cites here are not minor changes. These are absolutely massive societal shifts. The populations of these states are substantially smaller now than they otherwise would be. And not by a few thousand people: the changes here must be registered in terms of millions of people. The demographic realities of Kerala and Tamil Nadu have decisively changed—in large part by enhancing the agency of individual women.

## 4. FEMALE LITERACY AND SUSTAINABILITY

In Sen's account, there are fewer children born into a society with greater agency for women. But these children are more likely to live. The lives of *individual* children are given a boost by female literacy. The final comment I would like to make in this context is centered on the ecological implications of Sen's reflections. In Sen's account, greater agency for women has a very substantial impact on the earth and its life. There is an environmental dimension to primary schooling.

Sen develops the link between female education and the nonhuman environment in *The Idea of Justice*:

> Greater female education and women's employment can help to reduce fertility rates, which in the long run can reduce pressure on global warming and the increasing destruction of natural habitats. Similarly, the spread of school education and improvements in its quality can make us more environmentally conscious; better communication and a more active and better informed media can make us more aware of the need for environment oriented thinking.[18]

Here Sen notes a connection between female education and *sustainability*. The human relation to the earth is changed through greater agency for women. And if one asks "Why do population trends affect sustainability?" Sen's answer is clear. From an ecological point of view, more people lead to more resource consumption. An increasing human population will draw more from nonhuman life. On the other hand, a stable human population will not draw on nonhuman life to the same extent. The human effect on nonhuman species will be less severe—*if* the human population levels off. Moreover, the effects of this change will be even greater *if* this leveling off is coupled with practices that decrease resource consumption per person. The quest for more efficient and less destructive ways to meet our basic needs can be communicated through schools and fact based journalism.

## Sen, Rawls, and Locke

Sen and Rawls emphasize equality for women in their writings. Each thinker insists on primary schooling for all children. In point of fact, Rawls cites Sen's research on the effects of female literacy and employment roles on population growth at key moments in *The Law of Peoples*.[19] Rawls has adopted Sen's empirical claims here. And, while these points are absolutely critical in their own right, they are also connected to the stability of the international system. In particular, Sen and Rawls have replaced the concept of indefinite territorial expansion with the concept of sustainability. Stewardship of a society's territory, preserving its "environmental integrity"—not excessive population growth, the colonization of new lands and the destruction of wilderness—are the standards endorsed.[20]

From this point of view, the views of Sen and Rawls are radically divergent from the views of Locke discussed in the introduction.[21] Locke advocated for "Arms, Riches and Multitude of Citizens." He believed that the goal *of government* is to increase "numbers of man."[22] But Sen and Rawls have decoupled literacy, women's rights and sustainability from all discussions of state power. Domestic policy is not framed in terms of the strength of the state in the writings of Rawls and Sen.

Interpreted in this manner, the discussion in this chapter indicates the depth of the *internal* transformation that is needed to create a self-sustaining—non-expansionist—society. Education and basic rights for women must be a part of the system of institutions in *all* minimally just regimes.[23]

## NOTES

1. Rawls, *The Law of Peoples*, 50.
2. Ibid., p. 50.
3. Martha Nussbaum presents these problems in personal terms—through her narratives of Jayamma, Vasanti and other individual Indian women deprived of primary schooling—and through an analysis of society wide evidence, including the "literacy gap." For instance, Nussbaum notes that in India "in 1991, adult literacy rates for women were as low as 39 percent, as against 64 percent for men. In China, the figures are 68 percent for women and 87 percent for men." Nussbaum also notes how society wide averages can sometimes mask the depth of these problems. Adult literacy rates were 39 percent for women across India as a whole in 1991 but "in some rural areas female literacy is as low as 5 percent." Martha Nussbaum, *Women and Human Development*, 27-28.
4. "Babies can hear before they're born, starting around the beginning of the third trimester. At this stage, they can hear only loud sounds at medium to low pitches—like a car horn or a truck rumble—which is convenient because those are the sounds that most easily reach the baby through the insulation of the mother's belly. The mother's voice also reaches the baby's ears strongly because it is carried within her body . . . Auditory learning is already occurring during gestation. By the time they are born, babies prefer their mother's voice to a stranger's voice . . . They also prefer the sound of her language to a foreign language, probably because its cadence is familiar to them." Sandra Aamodt and Sam Wang, *Welcome to your Child's Brain*, 93.
5. "To understand a sentence, your child must know not only the meanings of individual words (called *semantic information*) but also how they relate to each other within the sentence (called *syntactic information*)." Ibid., 51. For more on the process of learning to read—and some potential challenges that hamper the development of reading skills—see 211-218.
6. Kwawe Anthony Appiah, *Cosmopolitanism: Ethics in a World of Strangers*, xii.

7. A person's self-interpretation is established, in large part, through the groups that person identifies with. For more on this theme see Sen, *Identity and Violence: The Illusion of Destiny*, 18-39.

8. This description of Sen is taken from Sen's self-description: "I can be, at the same time, an Asian, an Indian citizen, a Bengali with Bangladeshi ancestry, an American or British resident, an economist, a dabbler in philosophy, an author, a Sanskritist, a strong believer in secularism and democracy, a man, a feminist, a heterosexual, a defender of gay and lesbian rights, with a nonreligious lifestyle, from a Hindu background, a non-Brahmin, and a nonbeliever in an afterlife (and also, in case the question is asked, a nonbeliever in the fore-life as well)." Sen, *Identity and Violence: The Illusion of Destiny*, 19. Sen dedicated *The Idea of Justice* to Rawls.

9. Sen, *Development as Freedom*, 195. Sen notes that increasing female literacy also lowers the mortality rates for children in general *and* young girls; from this point of view, female literacy can reduce the number of "missing women" in a society. For more on these and other closely related themes see *World Development Report 2012: Gender Equality and Development*. The second chapter—"The Persistence of Gender Inequality"—is especially relevant in this context.

10. Sen, *Development as Freedom*, 197-198.

11. As of 2011, the literacy rate in India was 74.04 percent according to the *United Nations Human Development Report*. Also, the literacy rate for males was 82.14 percent while the literacy rate for females was 65.46 percent. The literacy gap is still in evidence.

12. Sen, *Development as Freedom*, 218.

13. Ibid., 217.

14. Ibid., 195.

15. This point can be framed in more general terms. According to the *United Nations Population Fund*, the human population reached one billion persons in 1800, two billion persons in 1927, three billion persons in 1960, and four billion persons in 1974. In 2011, the human population on the earth reached the seven billion persons mark. This is a phenomenal increase—but it would be much higher without some progress towards gender equality in the last fifty years. For more information on this and related themes, see www.unfpa.org/public.

16. Ibid., p. 222.

17. Ibid., p. 222.

18. Sen, *The Idea of Justice*, 249.

19. Rawls, *The Law of Peoples*, 9, 109-110.

20. Ibid., 8-9. Note the connection between *overpopulation, mass migration*, and *war* in these passages.

21. See the section on "security through expansion."

22. The expression is part of a larger passage that diminishes the value of nature: " . . . and the ground which produces the materials, is scarce to be reckon'd in, as any, or at most, a very small, part of it; So little, that even amongst us, Land that is left wholly to Nature, that hath no improvement of Pasturage, Tillage, or Planting, is called, as indeed it is, waste: and we shall find the benefit of it amount to little more than nothing. This shows, how much numbers of man are to be preferred to largnesse of dominion, and that the increase of lands and the right imploying of them is the great art of government." Locke, *Two Treatises on Government*, 297-298.

23. The ambiguity that exists in *The Law of Peoples* in regards to public health does not exist for primary schooling. A stable population requires primary schooling for all persons. In the absence of universal primary schooling and basic rights for women, the population of a society will continue to expand at an unsustainable rate—and ultimately cause instability and conflict in the international system.

# FIVE

# Employment

In the last three chapters, a simple message has emerged. In Rawls' view, the principles "one person one vote," "basic health care for all," and "mandatory primary schooling" are fair to individuals and useful to society. Experience has shown these principles work.

The positive message of section 5 of *The Law of Peoples* is clear. A society centered on the ideals of freedom and equality is very desirable. The harsher message of *The Law of Peoples* is also clear. Claims like "men can vote but women cannot" or "basic health care for children but not adults" or "primary schooling for boys only" are harmful to persons and society. Organizing political life around these claims is not ideal.

The contrast between the negative and the positive messages of *The Law of Peoples* is central to its meaning. The political character of a society depends in large part on its institutions and its leading principles. But the last feature of Rawls' model of equality I would like to comment on is his analysis of unemployment. In Rawls' view, the government of a liberal people must act as "the employer of last resort."[1] The long-term unemployment of persons in society is not just or fair.

Moreover, Rawls' perspective towards unemployment in section 5 of *The Law of Peoples* is not framed in terms of expanding the power of the state. Rawls does not say citizens must be productively employed—relative to the citizens of other nations. Economic nationalism is not part of the language used.[2] Rather, Rawls thinks about the impacts of unemployment on the lives of individuals—just as he examines the denial of health care and the exclusion from primary schooling in terms of the person. The indefinite expansion of state power is not the goal here.

## 1. HARM

Rawls believes employment is a condition of equality in the life of a people. A person with no chance of employment is not on an equal level with their employed peers. The key question, however, is "Why?" Why does Rawls hold such strong *political* views about a person's *economic* role?

To answer this question, consider the statement Rawls makes in chapter 5 of *The Law of Peoples*. Here Rawls claims that: "The lack of a sense of long-term security and of the opportunity for meaningful work and occupation is destructive not only of citizens' self-respect, but of their sense that they are members of society and not simply caught in it." [3]

In this passage, unemployment is not a "transitory pain" in Mill's sense of the word. Lacking a job is not like stubbing one's toe.[4] Instead, the loss of employment can lead to a wide range of problems. On an economic level, an unemployed person can be excluded from the goods circulating through society. The lack of a wage can cut a person off from a wide variety of markets. And over time, the inability to gain access to the goods circulating through society leads to insecurity and physical deprivation. The body of the unemployed person is directly threatened.

Unemployment quarantines the person from a variety of goods. Isolation from markets causes immediate harm. Unemployment, however, can also have a negative impact on the mentality of the person. The feeling of working together with others is lost when a person lacks an employment role. A recurring sense of accomplishment is no longer experienced. The sense of supporting one's self or one's family are also casualties of long-term unemployment. The thoughts and feelings of the person with no prospect of work are deeply affected.

Understood in this way, it is the range of harms that follows from unemployment that makes the removal of unemployment from society so important. Employed and unemployed persons in society lead very different lives.

*Food and Shelter*

Rawls associates unemployment with lasting negative effects in the life of a person. And it is probably relevant to note in this context that Rawls grew up in Baltimore during the Great Depression in the 1930s — at one point during this period, it is estimated that over 20 percent of the adult male working population in the United States of America was unemployed.[5]

In the Great Depression, millions of people lost their jobs through no fault of their own.[6] The 1930s stands out as one of the worst periods in the economic history of the United States of America. But Rawls does not leave his analysis of unemployment with this description of harm. There are several passages in *The Law of Peoples* that deal — directly or indirectly — with unemployment. Unemployment is one of many under currents in this text.

For instance, in chapter 15 of *The Law of Peoples*, Rawls draws out the connection between unemployment and the inability to gain access to food. In particular, he "notes" that: "there would be massive starvation in every western democracy if there were no schemes in place to help the unemployed."[7]

The claim in this passage is both harsh and direct. No employment, no income: no income, no food. The market for food — the fact that food has a price and must be purchased — can act as a barrier to food for the unemployed person.

Rawls draws a connection between unemployment and starvation. In the absence of social policy, large numbers of persons can be priced out of their lives. Nor is this observation limited to the market for food: the same point can be made about other vitally important goods. The ability of a person to pay rent, for instance, is threatened by unemployment: a person without an income is in danger of losing their home and shelter. Things such as clothing and transportation can also be priced beyond the reach of the unemployed person. The "all-purpose means" necessary to live become harder to secure.[8] And, again, the kind deprivations experienced here are not just physical in nature. How can a person make plans about the future while lacking these goods?[9] What opportunities are available to the person in this condition?

## 2. POVERTY

Rawls takes on the point of view of the victims of unemployment in *The Law of Peoples*. "How does an unemployed person experience society?" is the question Rawls implicitly asks. But I would now like to turn to some of Sen's reflections on poverty and hunger. Sen's concerns go beyond unemployment per se, and they are grounded in very precise empirical and historical analyses. However, he is cited by Rawls at key moments in *The Law of Peoples* and clearly influenced Rawls' thinking on these problems. Reflecting on these texts will further clarify Rawls' argument.

*The Great Bengal Famine*

Rawls raises the topic of famine at several points in *The Law of Peoples*. The starvation of persons is something every government must strive to prevent. But what is mentioned by Rawls is the central topic in many of Sen's writings. How does Sen think about famine?

In the text *Poverty and Famines: An Essay on Entitlement and Deprivation*, Sen challenges a misperception about the cause of famine. Famines do not necessarily occur because of an overall shortage of food. Instead, famines can occur if many of the poorest members of society lack the income and wealth and other "entitlements" necessary to gain access to food. Famines have *economic* and *political* causes in Sen's analysis.

To support this claim, Sen examines the "Great Bengal Famine" which broke out in British-administered Bengal in 1943. In this famine, two to three million Bengalis died of starvation or the diseases related to starvation over the course of a year.[10] The Great Bengal Famine was a truly monumental disaster: in Sen's estimation, one of the worst events in the history of Bengal. The cause of this famine, however, was not an overall scarcity of food. As Sen notes, the total amount of rice produced in Bengal in 1943 "was thirteen percent higher than in 1941, and there was, of course, no famine in 1941."[11] The cause of the Bengali famine cannot be traced back to a drop in this staple crop. Nor can the famine be traced to a sudden drop in the amount of wheat that was imported into the region. Sen notes that there was more wheat available per person in Bengal in 1943 than in 1941.[12]

"Food availability decline"—FAD in Sen's abbreviation—cannot explain the Great Bengal Famine. More food was available in Bengal in 1943 than in non-famine years. But what, then, did cause the famine to occur?

To answer this question, Sen turns to different sets of economic data. In particular, he looks into the behavior of rice prices in Bengal. Here is Sen's summary of this data:

> The wholesale price of rice, which had been between Rs. 13 and Rs 14 per 'maund' (82.3 lbs) on 11 December 1942, rose to Rs. 21 by 12 March 1943 and to above Rs. 30 by 21 May; by August it had risen to Rs. 37. Because of a government order fixing a maximum price, quotations for rice transactions are difficult to obtain from September 1943 onwards, but there are non-official reports of further rises, especially in retail markets, such as in October that rice was being sold in Chittagong at Rs. 80 per maund and in Dacca at Rs. 105 per maund. [13]

The evidence here is striking. The price of rice increased by almost 800 percent in parts of Bengal in the course of a year. There was a large bout of food inflation in Bengal in 1943. Another set of observations cited by Sen involves an economic description of the famine victims—in particular, the economic occupations of these persons. And here is what this evidence indicates: "The worse affected groups seem to have been fisherman, transport workers, paddy huskers, agricultural labourers, those in 'other productive occupations', craftsmen, and nonagricultural labourers, in that order." [14] As Sen notes, the feature that unites these groups is their poverty: almost all of the famine victims were highly impoverished rural Bengalis. [15]

These three sets of observations form the backbone of Sen's analysis. The total amount of food in Bengal did not drop in 1943. However, the rapid rise of the price of rice in 1943—coupled with the inability of certain groups of rural Bengalis to purchase rice at this higher price—is the immediate cause of the Great Bengal Famine.

### Political Economy

Food inflation is the proximate cause of the Great Bengal Famine. The story of the famine, however, does not end here. It is important to understand why the price of rice increased so much, so fast, in 1943. What events brought on this bout of food inflation?

Sen's answer to this question is exact and unsparing. The supply of rice in Bengal may have increased in 1943—relative to the 1941 level. However, the demand for rice and other goods increased even more because of "the war economy in Bengal." [16] In particular, Sen notes that "Bengal saw military and civil construction at a totally unprecedented scale" in 1943. And why were there such large and unprecedented public expenditures in urban Bengal in 1943? Because "the Japanese army was around the corner."[17] That is to say, the risk of a Japanese invasion—a risk that increased somewhat when Japan occupied Burma in 1942—set off a very hasty preparation for war by the British authorities in Bengal. Large sums of money suddenly entered into the Bengali economy. It was this injection of money into the Bengali economy that caused the price of rice and other goods to rise so fast.

The conclusion Sen draws from these economic facts is startling: "The 1943 famine can indeed be described as a 'boom famine' related to powerful inflationary pressures initiated by public expenditure expansion."[18] The "war boom" is what lies behind the Great Bengal Famine, not an overall drop in the food supply.

## 3. ENTITLEMENTS

The analysis in *Poverty and Famines* reveals the link between the market for food in a region and that region's political structure. The concept of "political economy" is crucial to Sen's analysis of famine. But the term Sen uses to highlight the interrelationship between political and economic phenomena is the term "entitlement." What exactly does Sen mean by this word?

In a key passage, Sen outlines the guiding intuition behind the "entitlement approach" to famine. Sen writes:

> A person's ability to command food—indeed, to command any commodity he wishes to acquire or retain—depends on the entitlement relations that govern possession and use in that society. It depends on what he owns, what exchange possibilities are offered to him, what is given to him for free, and what is taken away from him.[19]

There are many comments one can make about this passage. Without doubt a large number of rules—both written and unwritten—are at work in any exchange. But an analysis of the rules of exchange is exactly what is needed when explaining famine. Sen is honing in on the conditions that make possible the circulation of food in any society.

For instance, a fisherman might exchange the fish he catches for a large quantity of rice. And this may work most of the time. Fish will get the fisherman enough calories to live. But if the price of rice suddenly increases by 800 percent—as it did in parts of British-administered Bengal in 1943—selling fish for large amounts of rice calories will no longer work. The fisherman will not gain enough calories to live.[20]

In this situation, the activity of fishing has not changed. The fisherman is going about his business in 1943 just as he did in 1942 or 1941. However, when the price of rice increases by so much in a year, the value of the fish the fisherman owns has changed in the eyes of other people. The same fish will no longer command the same amount of rice in 1943 as it did in earlier times.

From this point of view, Sen is drawing attention to the conditional value of a good in a market. "Owning" a fish by itself does not establish the economic value of the fish. Instead, this value depends on 1) "owning" a fish and 2) "the exchange possibilities offered" for that fish. It is this more complicated sense of value that Sen is getting at with the term "entitlement relation."

### Pastoral Economies, Agricultural Laborers

The fisherman in Bengal suffered from an "entitlement failure." The story of the fisherman, however, has parallels in the lives of other people. A nomadic herdsman might sell an animal in exchange for large quantities of wheat. And this may work most of the time. But if the price of an animal suddenly falls—as when a drought forces many herdsmen to sell all of their animals at the same time (before these animals die of drought-related stresses)—the nomadic herdsman may be unable to buy enough wheat to live.

In this example, the grazing animal is like the fish. It is a good whose economic value depends on many other factors outside of the pastoralist's control. But this is not a hypothetical example. Sen shows how the sudden drop in the value of grazing animals owned by nomadic herdsman lead to the starvation of many of these persons in Ethiopia and the Sahel region of Africa. These persons did not die because there was no food to eat.[21] These persons died because the animals they owned could not be exchanged for the food that was available. The price of wheat was too high for these persons at this time.[22]

A pastoralist can suffer entitlement failure during a drought. But why might an agricultural laborer suffer food insecurity? Well, in "normal times," an agricultural laborer may gain an income by harvesting the crops of a landowning farmer. In this way, the laborer can gain access to enough money to purchase the food that is available. But if a flood destroys the landowner's crop, agricultural laborers can experience extreme deprivation. These persons become unemployed and lose their income. They can no longer earn enough money to purchase food. And in Sen's analysis, this kind of event led to the starvation of many persons in Bangladesh in 1974—"a year of greater food availability than in any other year between 1971 and 1976" in this country.[23]

### The Entitlement Relation and the Right to Food

Individuals can starve even when there is enough food to eat. Sen returns to this very grim point again and again throughout *Poverty and Famines*. But in the passage on entitlements cited above, Sen also speaks about goods that are sometimes "given for free." What does Sen mean by this phrase?

One way to interpret this phrase is to think about "the right to food." A government that affirms the right to food—that is, a government that affirms Article 25 of the Universal Declaration of Human Rights—has created an additional food entitlement in the lives of civilians. The person's ability to eat is not entirely dependent on the relative value of the goods she owns.

Or, to put this point in different terms: a person can sell fish or cattle to gain access to rice or wheat. A person can hand over some part of their wages to meet her calorie needs. And most of the time these exchanges will be successful in the sense that a person will gain enough food to live. But if there is an economic dislocation—or some other type of problem, such as a medical disability—a government that affirms the right to food has created practices to ensure the persons affected can survive. In this sense, a society where each person has a right to food, food is a good that sometimes must "be given for free."

### Entitlements and Human Rights

The analytical framework Sen creates in *Poverty and Famines* is distinctive. In Sen's anlaysis, the right to food is not a special metaphysical entity. Instead, the right to food is human in origin. A right to food is *a practice* that includes all persons in the circulation of food. A right to food is an extra form of entitlement to food in the person's life. [24]

*Poverty and Famines* is focused on the different ways a person can gain access to food in society. And within this perspective, a right to food opens up an additional route to food for the person. But the framework Sen develops in this text can apply to other rights besides the right to food. Food is not the only essential good in Sen's writings.

For instance, a person with a right to primary schooling and a right to health care can gain access to training and medical care—regardless of this person's economic status or the economic status of her family. The income of the parents or caregivers does not entirely determine the health care and training their child receives.

Understood in this way, a child whose rights are affirmed in society has an extra set of entitlements that goes beyond the income and savings and possessions of her family. This child receives a substantial boost from her society—as well as her family—in this situation.

## 4. RE-CREATING ENTITLEMENTS

The framework Sen develops in *Poverty and Famines* has implications for many terms of social analysis. For instance, in Sen's usage a family can be "poor" in the sense that each member of the family lives on less than two dollars a day. But this description of "poverty"—as important as it is—is radically incomplete. A person is also poor if they live in a society that does not affirm their human rights: not having access to primary schools; lacking basic health care; exclusions from basic goods such as food—these are also extreme forms of impoverishment in Sen's description.

The broader interpretation of poverty informs the title of Sen's monograph. The "poverty" in *Poverty and Famines* is not just referring to a meager income.[25] But the last comment I would like to make in this context concerns some of Sen's specific proposals for famine prevention. How does the notion of an entitlement feature here?

In *Development as Freedom*, Sen takes up the question of how famines can be prevented. He states:

> Since famines are associated with the loss of entitlements of one or more occupational groups in particular regions, the resulting starvation can be prevented by systematically re-creating a minimum level of incomes and entitlements for those who are hit by economic changes.[26]

And this could mean several things—including feeding persons in emergency camps. However, Sen draws attention to the use of a public employment program to prevent famine. He states: "Famines can be prevented by re-creating lost incomes of the potential victims (for example, though the temporary creation of wage employment in specially devised public projects), giving them the ability to compete for food in the market." [27] That is to say, employing individuals to complete a publicly useful project can prevent starvation. It can insure that individuals earn a wage that is sufficiently high enough to purchase the food that is available.

Sen highlights the ability of public employment programs to fend off famine. Nor are Sen's thoughts on public employment left in the abstract. A public employment program in Maharastra, India in 1973 re-created the entitlements of at least five million persons who were in danger of starving to death. [28] Dreze and Sen also noted that public employment programs helped to prevent a famine in Botswana, Burkina Faso, Ethiopia, Lesotho, Chad, and Uganda during the 1980s. [29] One of the largest potential disasters averted by the public employment route occurred in the Indian drought of 1987 "which could have lead to a very substantial famine given the disruption of the livelihoods of hundreds of millions of people." [30] Public employment also prevented a famine in China in the 1920's.

The upshot of these comments is clear. Public employment—government as the employer of last resort—is both humane to persons and useful to society. Justice and utility need not conflict with each other during an emergency. [31]

## NOTES

1. Rawls, *The Law of Peoples*, 50. Given the connection between famine and unemployment Rawls describes—as well as the wide range of harms caused by unemployment—one can argue that *all* societies must insure some type of employment role for their citizens. On this interpretation, decent hierarchical societies and benevolent absolutisms would be required to protect their civilians from persistent unemployment.

2. See the section on "Domestic Capture" in the Introduction.

3. Rawls, *The Law of Peoples*, 50.

4. "The happiness which (the philosopher's) meant was not a life of rapture, but moments of such, in an existence made up of few and transitory pains, many and various pleasures, with a decided predominance of the active over the passive, and having as the foundation of the whole not to expect more from life than it is capable of bestowing." Mill, *Utilitarianism*, 13.

5. Thomas Pogge identifies many links between the principles Rawls affirms in his political philosophy and Rawls' personal experiences. For instance, Pogge notes that Rawls' mother Anna played a prominent role in "The League of Women's Voters" movement in Maryland: Rawls indicated that his lifelong concern with feminism in his political philosophy had its origins here. Pogge also notes that "The most important

events in Jack's childhood were the loss of two younger brothers, who died of illness contracted from Jack." Thomas Pogge, *John Rawls: His Life and Theory of Justice*, 5.

6. "Problems with the operation of the gold standard and the unprecedented rise in unemployment were more than two notable aspects of the economic crisis of the 1930s. They were connected in ways that compounded and reinforced one another . . . Problems with the gold standard contributed directly to the collapse of output and to the increase in unemployment that begin in 1929." Barry Eichengreen, *Golden Fetters: The Gold Standard and The Great Depression*, 390.

7. Rawls, *The Law of Peoples*, 109.

8. Ibid., 50.

9. One of the mental effects of unemployment is a desire to emigrate. Rawls notes, for instance, that many Irish left British-controlled Ireland during the famine of the 1840s. Ibid., 9.

10. See Sen, *Poverty and Famines: An Essay on Entitlement and Deprivation*, 202 and *Development as Freedom*, 180.

11. Sen, *Poverty and Famines: An Essay on Entitlement and Deprivation*, 58.

12. Ibid., 60.

13. Ibid., 54-55.

14. Ibid., 72.

15. Ibid., 63-75.

16. Ibid., 72.

17. Sen, *Development as Freedom*, 167.

18. Sen, *Poverty and Famines: An Essay on Entitlement and Deprivation*, 75.

19. Ibid., 154-155.

20. For Sen's analysis of the plight of fisherman in Bengal, see *Poverty and Famines*, 67-68.

21. "There is . . . very little evidence of a dramatic decline of food availability in Ethiopia coinciding with the famine. Indeed, a modest increase in agricultural output for Ethiopia as a whole is recorded by the National Bank of Ethiopia for the famine years *vis-à-vis* the preceding years." Ibid., 92. The Sahel famines are more difficult to describe but they do not substantially change Sen's analysis. See 118-119.

22. Ibid., 99 and 120-121.

23. Sen, *Development as Freedom*, 165.

24. "The notion of human rights builds on our shared humanity. These rights are not derived from the citizenship in any country, the membership of any country, but are presumed to be claims *or entitlements* of every human being." (*italics mine*) Sen, *The Idea of Justice*, 143.

25. For more of Sen's thoughts on these problems, see chapter 4 of *Development as Freedom*: "Poverty as Capability Deprivation." In this text Sen describes poverty in terms of the *incapacity* to act. But this does not change the fact that "Human capability formation" always has at its roots the boost an individual receives through exchanges with other persons. A person's exclusion from the goods circulating through society *is* poverty in the most elemental sense.

26. Sen, *Development as Freedom*, 168.

27. Ibid., 168.

28. Sen, *Development as Freedom*, 180.

29. Jean Dreze and Amartya Sen, *Hunger and Public Action*, 115.

30. Ibid., 114.

31.  A broad description of the benefits of public employment programs is presented in *Hunger and Public Action*: "These (benefits) include: (1) being compatible with intervention at an early state of a subsistence crisis (when affected people are looking hard for alternative sources of income but do not yet suffer from nutritional deprivation); (2) obviating the necessity of movements of entire families to feeding camps; (3) at the same time, obviating the necessity of taking food to every village (as in a system of decentralized distribution), to the extent that the work-seeking adult population is mobile; (4) preserving family ties, particularly when employment can be offered near homes (without thousands of families being huddled together in relief camps); inducing positive market responses in the form of upward pressure on local wages; (6) allowing reliance on 'self-selection.'" Jean Dreze and Amartya Sen, *Hunger and Public Action*, 113-114. See also Sen, *Development as Freedom*, 177.

# SIX

## Summary of Part I

The preceding chapters have developed the argument in *The Law of Peoples* in greater detail. In Rawls' view, an international system of highly stratified states is very unstable. Diminishing extreme inequality in the international system is a critical goal in Rawls' analysis. However, the last four chapters have also made clear how complicated this task is. In Rawls' view, a society where elected representatives respond to the needs of the people establishes a framework for political progress. But this framework by itself is not enough to diminish extreme inequality. A liberal democracy must also affirm public health care institutions and a system of primary schools. Policies that create employment roles for all persons during emergencies are required. And a form of social safety net is needed for those who can no longer work—insuring each citizen has the "all purpose means" necessary to freely live.

Rawls' description of an ideal, liberal, society shows one way a people can diminish inequality.[1] A second point that has emerged in this discussion involves the contrast between Rawls and the political realist. From Rawls' point of view, the policy of "Arms, Riches and Multitude of Citizens" must be replaced. The indefinite expansion of state power is not Rawls' goal. Moreover, what is true for Rawls is true for Sen. Sen's feminism and thoughts about poverty are completely independent of any discussions of military power. Sen does not justify schooling and employment policies in terms of the strength of the state. Rather, the exchanges that occur in primary school are essential to what Sen calls "human capability formation."[2] Schooling develops a person's agency within society.

Similarly, the government of a society must protect the civilian population from a wide range of entitlement failures. This is a condition of each person's capacity to act.

Interpreted in this manner, Sen and Rawls are in very broad agreement when it comes to domestic policy, even though their theories are not identical in all respects. Civilians—not heads of state and the army—center the domestic policies of Rawls and Sen.

## NOTES

1. Many of the claims on page 50 of *The Law of Peoples* appear to be relevant for *all* minimally just regimes—even though a benevolent absolutism and a decent hierarchical society differ from a liberal society in many important respects. For more on this point, see chapter 2 note 11, chapter 3 note 18, chapter 4 notes 15 and 23 and chapter 5 note 1.

2. Sen, *Identity and Violence: The Illusion of Destiny*, 111.

# 2

# Foreign Policy

# SEVEN

## Reciprocity and Assistance

So far, I have been describing the ideal democracy in *The Law of Peoples* mostly through references to the social contract tradition. I would now like to look at Rawls' ideal democracy through the perspective of the Universal Declaration of Human Rights—first affirmed by forty-eight countries in 1948. What is the relationship between Rawls' text and this document?

Consider Article 25 of the Universal Declaration of Human Rights. Article 25 states the following:

> Everyone has the right to a standard of living adequate for the health and well-being of himself and his family, including food, clothing, housing and medical care and necessary social services, and the right to security in the event of unemployment, sickness, disability, widowhood, old age or other lack of livelihood in circumstances beyond their control.

The significance of Article 25 cannot be stressed enough. More than seven billion people live on the earth at this moment. But how many persons are actually protected from the deprivations described in this article? Have we created patterns of exchange—through our social and political institutions—that protect all the people of the globe?

When viewed in terms of Article 25, the social and political life of the nations of the world have a long way to go. Article 25 creates a sense of intense dissatisfaction with contemporary life. And from this point of view, Article 25 fits into a less used meaning of the word "ideal." It is not a utopian fairy tale. Creating a society that affirms Article 25 is possible and can be done. But it is also very far from becoming a reality for all persons everywhere. As Rawls might say: it is a principle that creates a goal—and thus a direction—for social policy.[1]

Article 25 establishes a new expectation in political life. Instead of just repeating what has been done, new patterns of exchange must be added to the ones that currently exist. The way food needs and health needs are met now is not good enough. But returning to *The Law of Peoples*, it is also clear that Article 25 is compatible with Rawls' description of the ideal democracy. Rawls' thoughts about health care overlap with the medical care promised in Article 25. Similarly, the need to ensure that individuals have access to "food, clothing and housing" is akin to Rawls' discussion of the essential goods necessary to freely live.

Moreover, if one broadens this comparison to include Article 23—which affirms "the right to work . . . and to protection against unemployment"—and Article 26—which affirms "the right to education"—and Article 7—"all are equal before the law"—and Article 18—"the right to freedom of thought, conscience and religion"—and Article 21—"universal and equal suffrage"—it becomes clear that a large part of Rawls' description of the ideal democracy in *The Law of Peoples* fits together with the actual commitments of existing societies around the world. That is to say: Rawls did not invent the principles he describes in *The Law of Peoples*. Instead, the Universal Declaration of Human Rights is part of Rawls' argument.

## 1. THE PREAMBLE

Rawls is explicit about the role of human rights in his text. He says at several points that his argument is compatible with the Universal Declaration of Human Rights. Nor is this influence limited to the articles of the declaration. The preamble to the declaration is also very important to Rawls.

This point can be made more precise. The last paragraph of the preamble states the following:

> The General Assembly Proclaims this Universal Declaration of Human Rights as a common standard of achievement for all peoples and all nations, to the end that every individual and every organ of society, keeping this Declaration constantly in mind, *shall strive by teaching and education to promote respect for these rights and freedoms and by progressive*

*measures, national and international, to secure their universal and effective recognition and observance,* both among the peoples of Member States themselves and among the peoples of territories under their jurisdiction.(italics mine)

There are many comments one can make here. For instance, the claim that the Declaration is "a common standard of achievement" is not hyperbole. It is based on the UNESCO "philosopher's report"—an empirical survey of the moral and ethical beliefs found in different cultures around the world.[2] But the clause I would like to focus on in this context is the clause that invokes "teaching and education" and "progressive measures." What might be meant by these phrases?

On one level, teaching and education involve an exchange of reasons. The evidence for a view is given in words. As such, teaching and education must be distinguished from physical coercion. Responding to an objection with evidence is not the same thing as the use of force.

Interpreted in this manner, the preamble is not making a claim in favor of cultural imperialism. The preamble is making a very simple statement. The reasons why human rights are so important to civilians must be shared. In particular, the idea that human rights protect civilians from heads of state and their armies is an idea that all persons everywhere should hear and consider.[3]

From this point of view, the preamble promotes an ongoing conversation or dialogue about political life. It asks the people of the world to exchange reasons with each other about the goals of the nation. On a second level, however, the preamble goes beyond the exchange of reasons and endorses the need for "progressive measures," that is, foreign aid that directly improves the lives of persons around the globe. And, while specific examples of these progressive measures are not given, there are possibilities. Helping a nation develop health care institutions— both medical and scientific—most definitely counts as a progressive measure. Advice on the drafting of a criminal and civil legal code might be a second example. Helping to fund a system of primary schools is a third possibility. Aid can also mean immediate humanitarian assistance including shelter and medicine, among other things.

From this point of view, the preamble helps to frame the foreign policy of a nation. Societies *can* generously give to each other. This *is* a human possibility. And what is so striking about *The Law of Peoples* is the way Rawls has incorporated these ideas into his account of a liberal democracy. A liberal democracy must observe and teach human rights through its conduct and policies; the foreign policy of the ideal democracy must affirm human rights. Rawls also advocates for what he calls "the duty of assistance"—a series of progressive measures that promotes human rights and the rule of law.[4] Words are not the only things peoples can share.

Interpreted in this way, *The Law of Peoples* shifts foreign policy away from the use of force, towards the stance of aid and beneficial exchange. An overwhelmingly nonviolent foreign policy is the message here.

*An Interpretation*

In Rawls' view, a foreign policy based on the Preamble is possible and can be done. There is nothing utopian about an exchange of reasons or the duty of assistance. However, the last section of *The Law of Peoples* is much more difficult to interpret than the first section of this book. The relations between nations are incredibly complex. And within this complexity, it is easy to get lost. What concrete steps must be taken to promote human rights—in the world as it is currently organized? How exactly should one interpret the duty of assistance—in the post-Cold War world?

This question can be put in different terms. It is one thing to describe a single ideal society. It is another thing to describe the relations between the 193 or so internationally recognized states on the planet. And it is even more difficult to think of each one of these states not as single unified entities but instead composed of different groups that may or may not be cooperating with each other. Even the very simplistic Machiavellian definition of a state creates many hurdles. Describing the political realities of a planet with more than one hundred armies and militias is no easy task.

A second point: existing political units are not static. There are groups within existing states that may wish to break off from the nation they are a part of and form a new state of their own. The political map as it currently exists does not capture this potential for change. Nor is this trend always towards more fragmentation. Several existing states may wish to unite in some ways to form a single, larger political entity. The sovereignty of existing states can be diminished in favor of a new superstate. There is also the problem of states without strong institutions and governments and the very terrible problem of civil war—which is, according to the Correlates of War database, the most common type of violent conflict since World War II.[5]

From this point of view, interpreting the duty of assistance is extremely challenging. How exactly should the duty of assistance be carried out, for instance, during a civil war? And the problem is not solely based on the variety of non-democracies around the world. One should also recall that *The Law of Peoples* is founded on a description of an *ideal* democracy. Actually existing democracies do not live up to this ideal in many respects. And thus the motives that inform the foreign policy of existing democracies is often guided by aims other than the promotion of human rights.

*Adjusting Democracy*

In responding to these questions, I will not directly follow Rawls' discussion of "nonideal theory." Instead, I will use some of the principles described so far to identify problems with political realism. This, I believe, follows the spirit of *The Law of Peoples*—even though I do not agree with all of the claims Rawls makes in Part III of his text.[6]

Moreover, I will not engage in the debate with cosmopolitanism that Rawls wades into. Instead, I will interpret the duty of assistance as *an adjustment* to the foreign policy of actually existing democracies—to move these democracies a little further away from political realism. This approach, I hope, will yield some important insights about foreign policy. And, most importantly, this approach is in line with the goal of protecting civilians.

## 2. DICTATION

I would like to begin this discussion with a few comments about the criterion of reciprocity discussed earlier. How might the criterion of reciprocity help identify problems in the international domain?

Rawls defines the criterion of reciprocity in the following terms:

> The criterion of reciprocity requires that, when terms are proposed as the most reasonable terms of fair cooperation, those proposing them must think it at least reasonable for others to accept them, as free and equal citizens, and not as dominated or manipulated or under pressure caused by an inferior political or social position.[7]

In this formulation, the criterion of reciprocity governs the public reasoning *within* an ideal democracy. Civilians and elected officials must respect the freedom and equality of all citizens when making a policy proposal. Rawls, however, also invokes the criterion of reciprocity in the context of foreign policy. The criterion of reciprocity must govern the relation *between societies*. The representatives of the ideal democracy need to reason with the other peaceful peoples in the world in a reciprocal manner.

Or, to put this point in different terms: the representatives of the ideal democracy cannot impose terms that are favorable to its own interests but highly unfavorable to the interests of its interlocutor. Instead, the policies it proposes must advance its own interest and be acceptable to other peoples. The *kind* of agreement is also important in the international domain.

So interpreted, the criterion of reciprocity places constraints on the reasons that can be used in international negotiations. Representatives of the ideal democracy cannot say to a peaceful state: "You will open your markets to our products . . . or we will invade your country." Nor can the ideal democracy say: "You must give up the sovereignty of your state and become a colony . . . or your citizens will be killed." These kinds of ultimatums are ruled out by the criterion of reciprocity.

Understood in this way, the criterion of reciprocity seeks to exclude the form of reasoning found in Thucydides' "Melian dialogue." If a militarily powerful state approaches a militarily weaker state and says "do this or else" the criterion of reciprocity is violated in the most extreme way imaginable. A people are forced to accept terrible terms.

## Political Realism, Further Defined

The contrast between a Rawlsian dialogue and the Melian dialogue could not be greater. When the representatives of militarily powerful Athens speak to the militarily weak Melians and say: "justice only exists between equals" and "the strong take what they can and the weak suffer what they must" the Athenians are relying on the larger size of their army to verbally pummel their antagonists into submission.[8] They are making a demand and threatening the Melians with invasion if they refuse. Nor is this a hypothetical story in Thucydides' account. The Melians did not give up their sovereignty to the Athenians and, as a result, the Athenians attacked the Melians and killed them in large numbers.

According to Thucydides, many of the women, children and other non-combatants of Melos were sold into slavery.[9]

The Melian dialogue is extraordinarily grim. When two states of very different military strength confront each other, the outcome can be extremely bad for the weaker state. But in addition to the immorality of it all—the Melian dialogue is, at its root, an example of the willingness to murder other people to achieve an "objective"—this dialogue draws attention to a key feature of political realism. In political realism, the larger size of one's army plays a decisive role in the relation with weaker states. That is, states with larger armies are more likely to get what they want. And the corollary of this principle is also clear. For the political realist, it is better to bargain from a position of military strength than a position of military weakness. When negotiating with a weaker army, one can face the situation the Melians faced.

## Negotiations without Armies

The argument sketched out here has proved compelling to many thinkers and heads of state. And it is true that one cannot simply trust the militarily strong states to do the right thing. But the immorality of classical political realism is really terrible to behold. Political realism can promote the selective use of invasion and murder as a matter of policy. It is the thing Machiavelli praised when discussing the actions of the king of Spain.[10] Moreover, classical political realism does not even lead to the security of the state that has adopted the policies of the political realist. If one state seeks to expand its power and territory, its neighbors will follow suit. And who is going to trust negotiations with a political realist?

The framework of political realism can lead to "conflict spirals."[11] And from an historical point of view, this pattern of escalating tensions and hostility has repeated itself many times. But returning to the positive argument of *The Law of Peoples*, one can say the following: for Rawls, the criterion of reciprocity indicates a second way. The terms proposed in a negotiation—between peaceful societies—must be acceptable to all involved *without* appeals to force. Consent between peoples can be achieved with no reference to the size of their armies.

Understood in this way, a fair negotiation cannot involve claims such as "Our army is stronger." This is unjust and immoral and sends exactly the wrong signal to the rest of the world.

### 3. TRUST

The criterion of reciprocity offers a second way of approaching a negotiation. Appeals to the size of one's army are not needed in a political
discussion. And this is not a minor point. This is an absolutely critical
distinction. All of the asymmetries that exist in regards to the armies of
states around the world—as well as the extraordinarily large differences
that exist between states in regards to military spending—should not
factor into the negotiations between peaceful societies. To do otherwise is
to create hostility out of thin air.

Interpreted in this way, the criterion of reciprocity promotes a mentality of inclusion between peoples with different military capacity. In
Rawls' words, the criterion "asks of other societies only what they can
reasonably grant without submitting to a position of inferiority or domination."[12] Moreover, when both sides understand that military threats
are not involved in the negotiation, anxiety is diminished. From this
point of view, the criterion of reciprocity is a de-escalating principle.

*A Newly Emergent State*

The criterion of reciprocity has a lot going for it. The habit of trust
between societies is the fruit of this ideal. But does the criterion of reciprocity also condemn nonmilitary uses of political power? Is a more restrained form of political realism ruled out by the criterion of reciprocity?

In reflecting on this question, it might help to examine a hypothetical
case.[13]

Consider a society that has just emerged from a colonial regime and
lacks primary schools, hospitals, and other essential institutions—because building these institutions was not the priority of the former colonial rulers. How should this new society be treated by other nations?

In the restrained form of political realism, the fact that this newly
emergent state lacks a powerful military does not mean it should be
invaded. The restrained form of political realism does not always use the
threat of military force to achieve its objectives. However, this version of
political realism has not given up on the basic goal of strengthening its
own economy and army. And it still views the relation between states in
anarchic terms.

In this situation, a "defensive political realist" might think there are
benefits to trading with the new regime.[14] In particular, a powerful state

might be able to meet its need for natural resources at a cheaper price through trade with the newly emergent state. In this way, the militarily powerful state can reduce the costs of various economic activities—and free up additional resources to strengthen its forces.

## Free Trade

The restrained form of political realism is more difficult to criticize than the classical political realism of Machiavelli or the ancient Athenians. Trade—in which each side freely exchanges a good they have for a good they want—is widely understood to be mutually beneficial. Moreover, it would seem as if free trade satisfies the criterion of reciprocity. It is an agreement that both sides willingly enter and does not involve the use of force.

On the surface, trade might seem to be fair and useful. But to understand what is problematic here, it might help to think more carefully about the political relation of the newly emergent state. What is the relation between civilians, heads of state and the armed forces in this post-colonial regime?

Let's assume for a moment that the newly emergent state in question is not a democracy. That is, there are no elections in this state—and a small group of persons and their families have indefinite control of the armed forces and the law making powers of the regime.

The fact that this newly emergent state is not a democracy has far reaching implications for the trade carried out with this state. If the newly emergent society is not a democracy—if it is, for instance, a military dictatorship or an intolerant religious monarchy or a police state—free trade *may* benefit the people in this regime. But it *may not*. It depends on what happens to the money the newly emergent state gains through trade.

If, for instance, the revenue gained through trade becomes the private property of the head of state—but does nothing to advance the core institutions of society, or help the people meet their basic needs—something has gone wrong. A small number of persons become incredibly wealthy. But these gains for these persons do not come with attendant gains in the lives of the people under their rule. Their gains through trade are private—not public—goods.

From this point of view, free trade can create extreme forms of inequality in the newly emergent state. Certain persons in the regime benefit massively. But if there is no way to share these benefits with the civilian population, a situation can arise where a very small minority have access to essential goods—while many civilians go without these goods and are subject to a wide range of insecurities. In this scenario, free trade does not promote human rights.[15]

## *The Trade in Weapons*

In the preceding example, a militarily strong state is exchanging money for the natural resources of a newly emergent state. The strong state can gain the resources it needs cheaply. And the newly emergent state gains a source of revenue. The question of what is done with this revenue, however, depends on other factors. It depends on *the political economy* of the newly emergent regime.

Exchanging natural resources for money is one type of exchange. But what if the kind of trade is altered a bit. What if the militarily stronger country is offering weapons in exchange for natural resources? What is the result of free trade in this situation?

Well, the initial outcome of this trade is quite clear. The military power of whoever owns the natural resources is substantially increased. These persons now have more weapons—and these weapons are probably more lethal—than the ones they had before. Moreover, the country of the defensive political realist is able to gain access to cheaper natural resources by exchanging less effective or older versions of the weapons it has already produced.

In this situation, both groups involved in the trade benefit from this exchange. But how are the people of the newly emergent regime doing? What is the effect of this trade in *their* lives?

Well, as was the case with the previous example, it depends. The people *may* benefit from this trade. Their lives *may* be made more secure from a foreign threat. But if the weapons are used by a military dictatorship to threaten or suppress the people in their state, the weapons trade has clearly had terrible effects in these persons' lives. And it is not just the civilians living in the military dictatorship who might be harmed. These weapons can be used to invade other countries. The civilians of neighboring states can become the victims of an expansionist war.

From this point of view, free trade may be uncoerced and mutually beneficial—for the specific groups involved in the trade. But when one looks at the consequences of this trade for the civilian populations affected by this trade, a very different picture emerges.[16] The trade "policies" of the defensive political realist can cause substantial harm.

### Denying Cooperation

The preceding examples do not indict trade per se. Trade can—under certain circumstances—promote human rights. But trade can also create extreme inequality in a society. It can make certain persons in the newly emergent regime extraordinarily wealthy. It can also hand over very powerful weapons to these persons and enable the most inhumane of goals.

From this point of view, the trade policies of the defensive political realist are too abstract to guide foreign policy. If trade gives the rulers of a military dictatorship the weapons they need to suppress their people— or the money needed to indefinitely maintain their power—something has gone very wrong with free trade.

It is at this point that one can see why Rawls does not frame the duty of assistance in terms of free trade. What is owed the newly emergent regime is not weapons or money. Instead, what is owed is highly specific aid—aid that promotes the rule of law and a political culture that respects human rights.[17] This is the kind of aid that helps *the people* of the newly emergent regime.

Or, to put this point another way, one can say: gaining weapons and money increases the power of a regime. But increasing the power of a regime does not determine how these powers will be exercised. Will heads of state use weapons to suppress the civilians living in their state? Will the riches of trade be used to build mega castles for the elite and their families? Blindly increasing the power of heads of state—without thinking about the political relation in that state and the political economy of that state—is a very great error.

Understood in this way, Rawls might advocate free trade with nations *after* they have developed decent or just political institutions. But for regimes that systematically and massively violate human rights free trade is not the best approach. Instead, pushing regimes *to change their political culture* is the thing most needed. It is *the political culture* of a society, in Rawls' view, that determines how the powers of that society will be used. And if an exchange of reasons is not successful—in Rawls' judgment, exchanging reasons with the heads of state of an outlaw regime is "unlikely to be effective"—the ideal democracy can "back up" their public criticisms with the "firm denial of economic and other assistance." The ideal democracy can also "refuse to admit outlaw regimes as members in good standing in mutually beneficial cooperative practices."[18]

### Alliances Between Democracies

The criterion of reciprocity is a de-escalating principle. When two groups follow the criterion of reciprocity in their negotiations with each other, a framework is created for an agreement that is both fair and mutually beneficial. Refusing trade, however, is more of a neutral stance. The refusal to trade involves a lack of agreement. But it is not a declaration of war or a preemptive strike. Taking hostile action and taking no action are not the same things.

The idea of refraining from trade and other mutually beneficial exchanges is very important to Rawls. Indeed, Rawls' use of the word "outlaw" fits in with this idea. An outlaw is a person who—because of their actions—is denied the benefits of society. Isolating *the heads of state* of an outlaw regime is Rawls' overarching position.[19] Still, the story cannot end with the denial of trade. Rawls makes clear that many different regimes around the world systematically violate human rights. He also assumes the existence of outlaw regimes into the future. And thus the ideal democracy's refusal of trade—by itself—does not prevent outlaw regimes from trading with each other. How should the ideal democracy respond to this possibility?

I find it interesting that Rawls speaks about alliances between democracies but spends very little time describing the alliances of non-democratic states. This may be an oversight on Rawls' part. But one possibility here is that Rawls believes the alliances between non-democratic states are extremely fragile. These alliances can quickly shift—as the interests of these regimes come to be defined in new ways.

For instance, at one point in his discussion of political realism, Rawls cites the nineteenth century British head of state Lord Palmerston. According to Palmerston, "England has no eternal friends and no eternal enemies: only eternal interests."[20]

The implications of Palmerston's quote are as clear as can be. The agreements between nations who have adopted the point of view of political realism can be broken at a moment's notice. These agreements are short-term conveniences, not lasting commitments. And this is, no doubt, why it is difficult to trust negotiations with a political realist. When a political realist says: "we will help you" the length and true price of this aid is never clear.

The question of how long an agreement will last is a crucial problem within the framework of political realism. And one must remember that from the perspective of political realism, strengthening a competitor state is always a risky decision.[21] But however this may be, Rawls *does* speak about the alliances of established democracies. He indicates that the alliances between established democracies are lasting because the institutions of these societies persist through time. More precisely, the relations between two ideal democracies remain positive—as long as these democracies affirm human rights in their practices and their political cultures.

From this point of view, the alliances between ideal democracies are more likely to persist. The political culture of these societies allows these societies to trust each other. And this is not just an abstract point, for theory alone. The lasting nature of democratic alliances is very beneficial to these democracies. There is a lot to be gained from cooperation.

In particular, the foreign policy of liberal democracies can be reliably coordinated with each other. Many democracies can, for instance, adopt the same stance towards a non-democratic regime. Equally important here is the time frame of these policies. Since the institutions of these ideal democracies are stable, the foreign policy of these democracies can remain fixed on the goal of promoting human rights. The denial of trade and assistance—*with heads of state and other elite of outlaw regimes*—can be maintained for an indefinite period.

From this point of view, the alliances between ideal democracies amount to a new form of collective action. Coordinated, intergenerational, foreign policy commitments are possible here.


## SUMMARY

In this chapter, the foreign policy of Rawls' ideal democracy has been sketched out in greater detail. In particular:

1. An ideal democracy must not appeal to force to settle negotiations with peaceful societies. In this way, nascent hostility between societies does not arise.
2. An ideal democracy can refrain from trade with the heads of state and other elite of regimes that violate human rights.

3. Ideal democracies can coordinate their foreign policy with each other. Several different democracies can refrain from trade with an outlaw state.

4. Ideal democracies can formulate and implement a foreign aid strategy in concert with each other.

Described in this way, the foreign policy of reciprocity and assistance is a foreign policy of nonviolence. *All* of the claims made here do not depend on the size or the power of a nation's army. And while some might think this policy is ineffective, Rawls would disagree. This type of foreign policy can be extremely effective. Isolating the heads of state of outlaw regimes is a very potent form of collective action. Military escalations are not the only way to respond to a problem.

## NOTES

1. Rawls, *The Law of Peoples*, 90.
2. For more on the UNESCO "philosopher's report" see Mary Ann Glendon, *A World Made New*, 73-78.
3. Rawls, *The Law of Peoples*, 27. For similar statements see 42, 79.
4. Rawls, *The Law of Peoples*, 5.
5. Jack S. Levy and William R. Thompson, *Causes of War*, 186. The chapter this quote introduces indicates just how difficult civil wars are to analyze and understand.
6. Most importantly, I do not agree with the idea of a "Supreme Emergency Exemption" which Rawls defends in *The Law of Peoples*. For more on the idea of a "Supreme Emergency Exemption" see Michael Walzer, *Just and Unjust Wars*, 251-283. For criticism of the "Supreme Emergency Exemption" see Stephen Nathanson, *Terrorism and the Ethics of War*, p. 146-159.
7. Rawls, *The Law of Peoples*, 14.
8. Thucydides, *The History of the Peloponnesian War*, 352. Note I have used the word "justice" in place of the translator's "right."
9. Ibid., 357.
10. "Nothing makes a prince so much esteemed as to carry on great enterprises and to give rare examples of himself. In our times we have Ferdinand of Aragon, the present king of Spain. This man can be called an almost new prince because from being a weak king he has become *by fame and glory* the first king of the Christians; and if you consider his actions, you will find them all very great and some of them extraordinary." (*italics mine*) Machiavelli, *The Prince*, 88. And what did Ferdinand do to earn such accolades? He waged war against his neighbors, initiated the inquisition and set in motion the process of colonizing the Americas. Machiavelli is the anti-Rawls.
11. A conflict spiral can be described within the more general framework of "the security dilemma": "If one's adversary is growing in strength or forming alliances, the inherent uncertainty about the adversary's intentions often leads one to conclude that the worst outcome is the failure to build up one's own power, leaving one's interests exposed if the adversary turns out to have aggressive intentions. States may take these

actions for purely defensive purposes, but adversary states often perceive these actions as threatening. Compounding this is the fact that most weapons systems can serve offensive as well as defensive functions. The result is a tendency toward worst-case analysis in the context of extreme uncertainty. The threatened state responds with measures to protect its self, and those measures are in turn perceived as threatening by the other. This can generate an action-reaction cycle and a conflict spiral that leaves all states worse off and that can sometimes escalate into war. This is the core of the *security dilemma*: actions that states take to increase their security often induce a response by adversaries and actually results in a decrease in their security." Jack S. Levy and William R. Thompson, *Causes of War*, 29-30.

12. Rawls, *The Law of Peoples*.

13. I have framed this hypothetical case to bring out features of defensive political realism. There are many, many other problems that one could focus on in this context. See, for instance, Thomas Pogge, *World Poverty and Human Rights*, 146-167.

14. Defensive political realism seeks to avoid situations of military weakness or inferiority relative to other states. Roughly speaking, this is achieved by maintaining a "balance of power" between different states. For more precise descriptions of "defensive political realism," see Jack S. Levy and William R. Thompson, *Causes of War*, 34-35 and the texts they cite.

15. "When we ask whether we are treating developing countries unfairly when we buy their resources at going world market prices, we will answer in the negative. In doing so, we are liable to overlook the far more important question of whether we are treating the poor populations of developing countries unfairly when we purchase their natural resources from their oppressors. The question is not what are we doing to developing countries. The crucial question is what are we and the rulers and elites of the developing countries *together* doing to their impoverished populations." Thomas Pogge, *World Poverty and Human Rights*, 23.

16. Pogge fiercely denounces "selling juntas and autocrats the weapons they need to stay in power." In his estimation, however, purchasing natural resources from non-democratic heads of states *is even worse*. See Thomas Pogge, *World Poverty and Human Rights*, 22.

17. In *Justice as Fairness: A Restatement*, p. 174, Rawls notes that the elected representatives of a liberal democracy must decide "what fraction of the social product" is needed to support the health care needs and educational needs of its people, within the context of other essential requirements, such as "retirement" and "national defense" and the maintenance of essential infrastructure. The implication is that a liberal society (1) has a surplus of social product and (2) uses part of this surplus of social product to fund essential policies and institutions. Within this framework, the duty of assistance is foreign *aid* (not a loan) that helps another society achieve the surplus of social product required to fund its essential institutions. As such, the duty of assistance obligates a liberal democracy to devote more of its own social product to foreign aid. This theme is taken up in greater detail in chapter 8.

18. John Rawls, *The Law of Peoples*, 93.

19. Humanitarian aid to civilians living under an outlaw regime is always permissible.

20. Ibid., 28.

21. See note 20 of the Introduction.

# EIGHT

# Political Economy

The alliances formed by political realists are constructed on shaky ground—since a political realist is always suspicious of his neighbor's power. Democratic alliances, however, are founded on the criterion of reciprocity and mutual respect. Two democracies are more likely to trust each other.

The distinction between democratic and expansionist coalitions is very significant. Democracies are better able to act collectively. The alliances formed by democracies are not plagued by anxiety and suspicion. But Rawls' affirmation of coordinated foreign aid—and collective defense—does have implications for the ideal democracy's political economy. The budget of the ideal democracy is directly affected.

Thus, in this chapter, I develop Rawls' concept of political economy in greater detail. The ideal democracy's funding priorities will be examined. Moreover, in developing Rawls' concept of political economy, I will draw on some of Sen's many and varied discussions of this topic. Political economy is a decisive theme in the foreign policies of Rawls and Sen.

## 1. THE BUDGET

I would like to begin this discussion with Rawls' concept of the national budget. How does the ideal democracy spend its funds?

To answer this question, consider Rawls' statement on political economy in *Justice as Fairness*:

> Observe that what sets an upper bound to the fraction of the social
> product spent on medical and health needs are the other essential ex-
> penditures society must make. . . . For example, an active and produc-
> tive workforce must be sustained, children must be raised and properly
> educated, part of the annual product must be invested in real capital
> and another part counted as depreciation, and provision must be made
> for those that are retired, *not to mention the requirements of national de-*
> *fense and a (just) foreign policy in a world of nation states.* The representa-
> tives of citizens who view these claims from the point of view of the
> legislative stage must strike a balance between them in allocating soci-
> ety's resources. (*italics mine*)[1]

In this passage, Rawls does not rank the spending priorities of a democratic society. Health care is not placed above other goals like the educating of children or national defense. Nor is health care placed below these
priorities. Instead, health care, the educating of children, foreign aid and
national defense—as well as the other objectives named in the passage,
including full employment—are *essential* goals. Each area must receive
part of the social product.

Rawls' initial statement on political economy establishes a plural
number of essential goals. Funding one objective only is a mistake. A
second comment: Rawls does not attach numerical values to these objectives. He does not claim that health care should consume 4 percent or 40
percent or 80 percent of the social product. Nor does he claim that national defense calls for some specific amount. Nothing precise is identified
here. However, what Rawls does draw attention to is the interconnected-
ness of spending objectives in the budgeting process. The commitment of
resources to one area *constrains* the total resources available to other do-
mains. The social product is not infinite in this passage.

The two points identified here—the claim that a society must fund a
range of goals, and the finite nature of the social product—indicate a
great deal about the ideal democracy. In Rawls' view, the elected representatives of a people must "strike a balance" when it comes to funding
society's essential priorities. The items of the budget are interdependent.
And this means the funds devoted to foreign aid and national defense
constrain domestic spending. Foreign policy and domestic policy must be
thought together.

*Voting for Foreign Aid*

The passage from *Justice as Fairness* sheds new light on foreign aid. Representatives must include burdened societies in their spending decisions.[2] And it is not just the representatives of the ideal democracy that must adopt this priority. The citizens living in the ideal democracy must understand the reasons why the duty of assistance is so important and vote for this goal. Ultimately, the citizens of the ideal democracy create the mandate for foreign aid.

Interpreted in this manner, the duty of assistance is not a statement of moral principle that comes from on high. It is the beliefs of the citizenry — and the decisions made by the elected representatives of the citizenry — that ultimately funds foreign aid. The needs of distant neighbors are understood.

*The Defense Budget*

The duty of assistance has its roots in the beliefs of the people. The ideal democracy is not totally absorbed in its own existence. And, while Rawls does believe in a possible future without the duty of assistance, the basis for this claim is not the waning interest of the ideal democracy. Rather, Rawls believes burdened societies can develop politically and economically. All civilians can live under the rule of law.[3]

The duty of assistance is a core element of Rawls' foreign policy. The citizens of the ideal democracy fund foreign aid for as long as it is needed. But how does national defense effect the budget of the ideal democracy? What role does Rawls give to military spending?

In the passage cited above, Rawls speaks about national defense "in a world of nation states." Defense spending and the nation state are linked together. And the reason for this connection is clear. Spending on national defense is necessary *because* there are outlaw regimes.[4] The reality of states with armies, possessing lethal weaponry, headed by persons with little regard for human rights, alters the political economy — and the political culture — of the ideal democracy.

Interpreted in this manner, Rawls' discussion of national defense parallels his discussion of the duty of assistance. Outlaw regimes *obligate* expenditures on national defense just as burdened societies *obligate* expenditures on foreign aid. Outlaw regimes and burdened societies cannot be ignored.

*The Lower Bound of Defense Spending*

The parallel between the duty of assistance and national defense is very important. A democracy cannot neglect threatening nation states—anymore than it can pass over the realities of extreme poverty and ineffective government. There is a wide range of problems foreign policy must address. Rawls treatment of national defense does, however, differ from his treatment of foreign aid in one critical respect. Rawls speaks openly of a future without burdened societies. He is hopeful when it comes to questions of development and the rule of law. However, Rawls never makes this point about the armed forces. Military spending does not dwindle towards zero in *The Law of Peoples*.

From this point of view, Rawls is somewhat pessimistic when it comes to outlaw regimes. Powerful outlaw regimes are deeply entrenched in Rawls' political philosophy. And this has significant implications for *The Law of Peoples*. The ideal democracy must respond to the threatening states that exist now—as well as the threatening states that might, one day, exist in the future. National defense is not a transitional priority from Rawls' point of view.

*A Nuclear Arsenal*

Spending on the armed forces is a deeply rooted need in political life. The armed forces will always claim some part of the budget. And the reason for Rawls' caution here is very clear. The ideal democracy must avoid a condition of excessive military weakness—relative to the expansionist states of its time. The ideal democracy cannot neglect its armed forces.

Rawls seems resigned to military expenditures. There is a lower bound to defense spending underneath which the ideal democracy cannot go. And it is important to recall Rawls' commitment to a nuclear arsenal in this context. The ideal democracy must spend part of the social product on nuclear weapons.

From this point of view, the ideal democracy is changed by the existence of outlaw regimes in a fundamental way. Outlaw regimes introduce an objective into the ideal democracy that is radically at odds with the duty of assistance. Nor is the decision to fund a nuclear weapons program restricted to the upper echelons of the government. Rawls' ideal society is a democracy—and its citizens participate in the political process. On some level, the citizen of the ideal democracy understands and affirms the commitment to a nuclear arsenal.

## The Upper Bound to Defense Spending

Rawls identifies a hard lower bound in regards to military spending. There is a need for the ideal democracy to avoid situations of excessive military weakness—relative to an expansionist state. But what about an upper bound to spending on national defense? Does Rawls cap the total amount a democracy devotes to its armed forces?

From one point of view, the answer is "No." Spending on national defense is linked to the threats posed by outlaw regimes. And if the threats posed by these regimes are large, the amount of social product devoted to national defense must be large, too.

To cite the most extreme example presented by Rawls: during the early years of World War II, "the nature and history of democracy and its place in European history were at stake."[5] Democracy itself was in danger of being extinguished. And this possibility is critically important for assessing Rawls' foreign policy. The defense expenditures of societies in these circumstances *must* be high. The danger posed to democratic and decent societies in World War II was extraordinarily large.

## The World State

There is no precise upper bound to military spending in *The Law of Peoples*. "It depends on the circumstances" might be Rawls' response to this question. It is a mistake, however, to conclude from Rawls' unwillingness to identify an upper bound to defense spending that the *The Law of Peoples* has nothing more to say on this matter. Rawls does not believe military spending is an end in itself. Rawls is not a militarist in any sense of this word.

Or, to put this point in different terms: Hitler's regime engaged in war with several nations. The creation of a "world state"—or something like it—seemed to be a part of Hitler's goal. However, the creation of a "world state" requires a ruler to embark on an extended period of economic and military expansion.[6] Conquest cannot be achieved with thoughts alone. As a result, substantial amounts of the social product must be siphoned away from other vitally important social goals and redirected to military purposes—*before* war is actually waged.

Interpreted in this manner, the creation of a world state requires an indefinite expansion of a society's economic and military power. The political economy of a state seeking global domination is totally warped. But the ideal democracy, which has given up on the desire to expand its territory, does not need to indefinitely increase its wealth.[7] Nor does it need to continuously direct massive amounts of the social product to its armed forces. The ideal democracy is not consumed by these goals. As a result, the ideal democracy can revert back to a more balanced political economy in times of peace.

The contrast between the world state and the ideal democracy draws attention to the deepest strand of Rawls' thoughts about military expenditures. Rawls does not identify an upper bound to defense spending. But since the ideal democracy does not seek to expand its territory—and does not need to continuously upgrade its armed forces to achieve this goal—the ideal democracy's political economy in peace looks very different from its wartime posture. Planning and preparing for war are not "ends in themselves."

## 2. A COMPARATIVE APPROACH TO POLITICAL ECONOMY

The contrast between the ideal democracy and the world state goes to the heart of *The Law of Peoples*. The ideal democracy has banished the fantasy of the world state from its political culture. And when one broadens the perspective to include the duty of assistance, the gulf separating these two points of view becomes even greater. A representative of the ideal democracy sees a burdened society and offers aid. A political realist sees a burdened society as an opportunity for conquest and expansion. There are few chasms in political life as wide as this.

The world state is anathema to Rawls. An effective world state— where one person commands a global army—is a nightmare of total control. But what, one may ask, is *Sen's* view of political economy? And how does Sen analyze spending on the armed forces?

Sen's approach to political economy is similar to Rawls' approach to political economy in the sense that it is founded on careful comparisons between different societies. Both Rawls and Sen use a "comparative method." But whereas Rawls contrasts the *ideal* democracy with the expansionist states of World War II, Sen's comparisons never make reference to an ideal society. Sen's comparative method is historical in a deeper sense.

*Political Economy in China*

Sen's approach to political economy involves a careful set of comparisons between actually existing societies. Sen never uses the concept of the ideal society in his analysis. But to better understand Sen's method it will help to look at some of his examples in greater detail. How does Sen describe the political economy of some actual states?

Consider Sen's discussion of the massive famine that broke out in China from 1958-1962. It is estimated that thirty million persons died in this catastrophe.[8] But in analyzing the causes of this famine, Sen hones in on the mistaken information the Chinese leadership had about conditions on the ground in rural parts of the country. In Sen's recounting:

> The vast number of communes or cooperatives who had failed to produce enough grain, of course, were aware of their own problem. But thanks to the widespread news black-out they did not know anything much about the widespread failure across rural China. No collective farm wanted to acknowledge that it alone had failed, and the government in Beijing was fed rosy reports of great success even from the badly failing collectives. By adding up these numbers, *the Chinese authorities mistakenly believed they had one-hundred million more metric tons of wheat than they actually did,* just as the famine was moving towards its peak.[9]

One-hundred million metric tons is a gigantic amount of grain. It is more than two trillion pounds of wheat. The scale of this misinformation is truly incredible.

The famine of 1958-1962 is the product of a colossal blunder. As Sen notes, *Mao himself* blamed the famine on the inability of the Chinese leadership to gain access to accurate information.[10] But this failure of the regime in regards to feeding its people does not mean the regime was incapable of pursuing objectives. Mao's regime began work on its nuclear weapons program in the 1950s and remained committed to this project during the famine.[11] And as Sen notes elsewhere, the development of a nuclear weapons program is not a trivial commitment. A large amount of resources, training and expertise is required to pursue this objective. A state foregoes a great deal to build "the bomb."[12] But even this assessment does not fully capture the realities of the situation. Mao's army occupied Tibet in 1949, entered the Korean War in 1950, fired at islands in the Taiwan Straits in 1954 and 1958, and was hostile to India throughout this period—finally attacking the border region in 1962. The communist regime was quite active in regards to military matters during the 1950s and 1960s even while the leadership was oblivious to the ongoing famine.

*Political Economy in North Korea*

Mao was focused on the military power of the Chinese state throughout his rule. A potent military was very much at the forefront of his decision-making. However, when one goes down the grim list of famines Sen analyzes in the twentieth century, it becomes clear that the distorted priorities of Mao's regime is not an isolated event. Just the opposite: it is a recurring pattern. Military spending and the history of famine are often linked together.

Consider Sen's comments about North Korea. North Korea is one of a handful of states that currently belong to the "famine league."[13] But what, exactly, is happening in this nation? Why did—and why are—North Korean civilians dying from lack of food?

In Sen's forward to the book *Famine in North Korea: Markets, Aid, and Reform*—written by Stephen Haggard and Marcus Noland—Sen notes that "the roots of the famine extend deeply into politics and cannot be assessed through economic analysis alone."[14] In particular, Sen notes that:

> . . . the rulers clearly were quite firmly distanced from the misery of their subjects. The priority of the military was strong, regional diversities were very considerable, and the official faith in a centralized food distribution system remained strong even as it crumbled all around. . . . Given the authoritarian nature of the government, there was no way of making the rulers change track, nor of course, any hope that the rulers with fixed views and priorities would make way for a different government.[15]

The claims in this passage hone in on the political economy of the North Korean state. There are no competitive elections in North Korea. As a consequence, civilians cannot replace the regime that has failed it so badly. The civilian population is stuck with the "military first" strategy of Kim Jong Il—and now his son.

The regime has given priority to the military in its spending decisions and cannot be voted out of office. These are key factors in the famine. But

Sen also alludes to the "regional" nature of the famine. What is meant here?

In chapter 2 of Haggard and Noland's text, attention is drawn to the caste system the North Korean regime implemented at the beginning of its existence. This system created a division between "core," "wavering" and "hostile" classes. As Hagard and Noland point out:

> . . . families of workers, soldiers, or party members were considered core; families of middle peasants, traders and owners of small businesses were considered wavering. The government classified twenty-nine distinct groups as hostile, from families of rich peasants, to individuals with clear religious identities, to the intelligentsia and even returning Chinese and Japanese Koreans.[16]

The caste system divided up North Korean society in an entirely new way. A permanent underclass was created at the state's inception. But this is not all. A second feature of this caste system is the geographic distribution of the citizenry it helped to create. In particular, the regime settled these groups in different regions of the state, with "core" members tending to reside in Pyongyang while "members of the hostile class were relocated to remote parts of the country."[17] Needless to say, the outlying provinces in the northeast—well removed from Pyongyang— were hit the hardest by the famine.[18]

The North Korean regime created a permanent underclass within the state. It lacks elections and is authoritarian, controlling where people live and how they gain access to food. But at the root of the regime is the "military first" strategy of the Kim family. This policy involves the maintenance of the fourth largest standing army in the world with over a million soldiers. The "military first" strategy also involves a commitment to the country's nuclear weapons program—which was initiated in the late 1950s—as well as the use of scarce foreign reserves to purchase military equipment abroad.[19] There is a massive distortion of priorities here.[20]

## *Military Spending in Other Famines*

The famines in North Korea and China in the twentieth century occurred during periods of high military spending—including spending on a nuclear weapons program. But even when the occurrence of famine is not bound together with the commitment to a nuclear weapons program, the issue of prioritizing military spending over other social goals is still very much in evidence. Sen notes that the regimes in Ethiopia, Somalia, Bangladesh, and Sudan were all "military dictatorships" at the time famines broke out in these nations.[21] It is pretty clear what this means. Even the Great Bengal Famine, discussed earlier, is rooted in military spending. The British authorities in Bengal did not lack the resources to direct food to starving Bengalis. Instead, the attention of the British colonial regime in Bengal was fixated on the Japanese army in nearby Burma. Military preparation can foster a fatal oblivion to impoverished civilians.

### 3. DIFFERENT PROBLEMS

Sen's analysis reveals a recurring pattern in political economy. Non-democratic regimes can direct large amounts of the social product to the military *during a famine*. Military spending and planning just goes blissfully on. But if one asks the question "Why did these regimes give priority to military objectives?" the answer does not seem to be a desire for world control. None of the regimes have identified the world state as their objective.

These comments draw attention to a difference between Sen and Rawls when it comes to political economy. Sen and Rawls both condemn run-away military spending. However, their analyses of military spending carry them in different directions. Rawls is focused on the preparation for war in the states that initiated World War II. The pattern Sen has unearthed, however, is not connected to the creation of the world state. Other factors are at work here.

### *The Global Arms Trade*

Sen draws attention to the warped political economies of non-democratic regimes. Giving priority to the armed forces is a recurring pattern in the history of famine. But how does Sen think about the military spending *of existing democracies*? What analysis is provided here?

When it comes to democratic defense spending, Sen highlights a different historical pattern. In particular, when Sen speaks about the sale of conventional weapons in his book *Identity and Violence: The Illusion of Destiny*, he notes that: "the principal suppliers of armament in the world market today are the G8 countries, which are responsible for 84 percent of the arms sold in the period between 1998 and 2003."[22] Moreover, not all the countries within the G8 participate in these exchanges: whereas Japan contributes nothing to the global arms trade, "The United States alone was responsible for about half of the arms sold in the world market, with two-thirds of its exports going to developing countries, including Africa."[23] The richest democracies on the planet—including the United States—play a leading role in the international market for arms.

Sen is very clear about the negative effects of the sale of weapons to developing countries. As noted in the previous chapter, the exchange of weapons with developing countries can have negative consequences for the civilians living in those states. The political relation is distorted—as rulers now have access to more lethal weapons than they did before. But this analysis can now be pushed a bit further. When a newly emergent regime decides to purchase weapons from an established democracy, it is not spending that money on education and health care. Development goals are crowded out by weapons purchases.

From this point of view, a weapons sale constrains spending on education and health care in a newly emergent regime. But even this observation understates the case. One must also consider the signal that is sent to the neighbors of the state that is receiving these weapons. What might *they* be thinking? And it does not take much to see how these leaders might be worried. "Why"—these persons might ask—"is my neighbor purchasing incredibly lethal arms?" "What"—they might wonder—"is my neighbor planning to do with this new capability?" And if these neighbors are sufficiently alarmed, they might decide to spend more on their own armed forces. The sale of weapons can have a cascading effect, as neighboring states feel constrained to devote more resources to their military budgets.

Understood in this way, an arms sale does not alter the political economy of one state only. The political economy of a state's *neighbors* can also be affected by this purchase. Adjacent states might devote more of the social product to their armed forces. And if adjacent states make a decision to spend more on their armed forces, less money is available to fund education and health care. The budget priorities of an entire region can become severely warped.

*Rebalancing*

Sen is highly critical of the policy of selling arms to developing countries. In Sen's analysis, the political economies of several nations are simultaneously distorted by a weapons sale. And this is not a mysterious
outcome that is hard to discern. The pattern, here, is quite predictable.
Few countries want to be a position of military weakness—relative to
their neighbors. If one state gains in military strength, pressure is put on
adjacent states to follow suit.

The preceding comments draw attention to a core insight of Sen's
foreign policy. Sen is highly critical of the status quo when it comes to
military spending in general and the global weapons trade in particular.
The best situation, Sen notes, is not one in which impoverished nations
race against each other to develop their military powers. Instead, developing nations need to *reduce* their military purchases and focus on providing education and health care to their peoples. A coordinated rebalancing of social expenditures is needed here.

Sen is clear about the approach the leaders of a developing country
should take towards their budget. As Sen puts it in *Development as Freedom*, austerity as a budgeting principle is best aimed at military expenditures:

> What really should be threatened by financial conservatism is the use
> of public resources for purposes where the social benefits are very far
> from clear, such as massive expenditures that now go into the military
> in one poor country after another (often many times larger than the
> public expenditure on basic education or health care).[24]

But belt tightening in regards to military expenditures in developing
countries is not the only thing needed. Belt tightening in regards to weapons production and the sale of weapons is also required. The revenue
gained through the arms trade is more than dirty.

*A Military Spending Cap*

So far, Sen's analysis has revealed two critical historical patterns. The
first pattern involves the tendency of non-democratic regimes to focus on
military build-ups while failing to meet the food needs of their own civilian populations. The second pattern involves the global arms trade,
which results in national and regional patterns of excessive military
spending.

In Sen's analysis, both patterns are producing terrible outcomes. Civilians around the world are bearing the brunt of these distortions. An immediate change of course is needed here. And, while Sen diagnoses two additional historical patterns involving the Cold War in Africa and nuclear proliferation in South Asia—which are discussed in the next chapter—the broad outlines of Sen's foreign policy have started to appear. In particular, Sen indicates a strong desire to lower military expenditures in *all* societies. The sum total of military expenditures—the upper bound of each society's military spending—needs to be reduced. But the nature of this cap is such that it must apply to all nations simultaneously. Developing countries must constrain their military purchases. Likewise, nations that sell arms in the global market must reduce their sales. And both steps need to take place at the same time. If one nation continues to sell arms to a willing buyer a pattern of military overspending can begin anew.

*Nuclear Escalations*

Sen's analysis lays the groundwork for a coordinated reduction in military spending. When it comes to military spending the political economies of the world are interlinked. But does Sen believe a society must devote part of its social product to a nuclear arsenal? How does Sen approach *this* question?

This issue will be addressed at length in the next chapter. However, a key element of Sen's analysis of nuclear weapons has already come to light. When a nation increases its military power it pressures other nations to follow suit. But what is true of conventional military power is also, Sen says, true of nuclear weapons. As soon as one nation develops a nuclear weapon, other nations will follow. The construction of a single nuclear bomb is an act of incredible hostility.

Sen develops this analysis in the context of South Asia and the conflict between India and Pakistan. But it also applies to some of the states discussed in this chapter. As noted earlier, Mao's regime in 1954—and the North Korean regime in 1956—decided to pursue a nuclear weapons program. But these choices did not appear out of thin air. These choices were also rooted in the policies of the Truman and Eisenhower administrations, as well as the legacy of the Cold War. There was a broader context of hostility underlying these decisions.

In particular, Truman used atomic weapons on the civilian populations of Hiroshima and Nagasaki in 1945, ending the lives of thousands
of Japanese citizens in an instant. And, as David Holloway points out—in
his article "Nuclear Weapons and the Escalation of the Cold War"—
Truman also threatened to use an atomic bomb at the beginning of the
Korean War. In particular Holloway draws attention to a press confer-
ence Truman held on November 30, 1950, where "Truman created the
impression, in answer to a reporter's question, that the atomic bomb
might be used in Korea at General Douglas MacArthur's discretion."[25]

Truman used the atomic bomb in the war against Japan and gave the
impression of considering the use of the atomic bomb in the Korean War.
Truman left office in January of 1953, but Holloway quotes President
Eisenhower telling the National Security Council on March 31, 1953 that:
"the taboo surrounding the use of nuclear weapons would have to be
broken." Holloway also notes that: "The Eisenhower administration
dropped hints that it would resort to nuclear weapons to bring the Korean War to an end, and it deployed nuclear weapons to Guam. Eisenhower later claimed that it was the threat to use the bomb that made possible
the armistice signed on July 27, 1953."[26]

Eisenhower and Truman both threatened to use atomic weapons in
the Korean War. It does not take much to see how these threats could
strengthen the resolve of Mao—and, later on, the Kim regime—to possess
nuclear weapons. But this was not the only moment in the early 1950s
where the American president considered nuclear weapons. Holloway
also notes that Eisenhower used a similar strategy of nuclear brinkmanship in the crises of the Taiwan Straits. In Holloway's description, this
conflict:

> . . . concerned the islands of Jinmen and Mazu (Quemoy and Matsu),
> which lie only a few miles off the coast of China and were still con-
> trolled by the Chinese Nationalist government in Taiwan. In 1954 and
> 1958, the Chinese Communists bombarded the islands with artillery.
> Eisenhower concluded in each case that the defense of Taiwan required
> the offshore islands be held. He was willing to use nuclear weapons if
> they were attacked, and he made that clear in March 1955 and August
> 1958. These threats were not a bluff. Eisenhower gave serious consider-
> ation to the possibility of using nuclear weapons.[27]

Clearly, these are complicated events that can be described in different
ways. Still, one must ask here: what signal did Truman and Eisenhower

send to Mao, the North Korean regime—and the Soviet Union—through these actions and statements? How, exactly, did Truman and Eisenhower expect these states to respond?

The policy of the Truman and Eisenhower administrations clearly played some role in the nuclear aspirations of the Mao and Kim regimes. And on a deeper level, Eisenhower's strategy of nuclear brinkmanship became established as a precedent for negotiations and was later repeated—consciously or unconsciously—by Khruschev. When Khruschev said: "I think the people with the strongest nerves will be the winners" and "The people with weak nerves will go to the wall" he was signaling his adoption of nuclear brinkmanship as an acceptable strategy of negotiation.[28] It is the Melian dialogue all over again—but this time with a psychological twist. Whoever has the strongest *nerves* will win. And in point of fact, the extraordinarily dangerous Cuban Missile Crisis in 1962 was fueled by the willingness of Khruschev and Kennedy to adopt the same pressuring posture towards each other—with the use of nuclear weapons acting as the stick. It was an extremely dangerous situation. At the time of the Cuban Missile Crisis, the United States possessed close to twenty-seven thousand nuclear weapons while the Soviet Union possessed close to three thousand.[29] The whole of humanity was at risk.

From this point of view, one can see why Sen analyzes *nuclear proliferation* in much the same way as he analyzes *conventional military escalations*. The use of the atomic bomb at the end of World War II initiated a pattern of response and counter response, as different states sought to acquire this weapon and gain leverage over their adversaries through its possible use. Stalin gave the order to create the Soviet atomic project two weeks after the bombing of Hiroshima.[30] Proliferation and the history of "the bomb" go together.

## SUMMARY

Drawing together the claims of this chapter, one can say the following:

1. The ideal democracy must allocate a finite social product to a diverse number of essential goals—including the duty of assistance and national defense.
2. Rawls establishes a lower bound to defense spending. There will never be a time when spending on national defense reaches zero.

3. Rawls does not establish an upper bound to defense spending. However, the ideal democracy is not continuously preparing for an expansionist war. As a consequence, the ideal democracy can revert back to a more balanced political economy in times of peace.

4. Sen affirms the principle of austerity in regards to military expenditures. Less of the social product must be spent on the armed forces in developing countries. The sale of arms globally must also be sharply curtailed.

## NOTES

1. Rawls, *Justice as Fairness: A Restatement*, 174.

2. Rawls, *The Law of Peoples*, 106.

3. Ibid., 111.

4. Ibid., 26.

5. Ibid., 99.

6. Ibid., 48.

7. Ibid., 107. Rawls and Mill both reject the idea of indefinitely maximizing the wealth of any society, or any class of society.

8. Hagard and Noland, *Famine in North Korea*, 7.

9. Sen, *The Idea of Justice*, 344.

10. Ibid., 344.

11. Differences of opinion about China's nuclear program created a rift between the Soviet Union and China as early as 1954. As Shu Guang Zang notes: "Moscow had sent a group of geologists to China to prospect for uranium early in the 1950s. Partly because of that, in his 1954 talk with Khruschev, Mao requested Soviet assistance for China's atomic weaponry program. To the Chinese leader's disappointment, Khruschev refused. . ." *The Cambridge History of The Cold War*, Volume I, Origins, 359. Among other things, this episode illustrates the headwinds confronting alliances between political realists.

12. Sen, *The Argumentative Indian*, 259-260.

13. Sen, *Development as Freedom*, 16. Haggard and Noland—drawing on the estimates of others researchers—believe six hundred thousand to one million persons died of starvation or starvation-related illness between 1994 and 2000. Haggard and Noland, *Famine in North Korea*, 76.

14. Haggard and Noland, *Famine in North Korea*, xviii

15. Ibid., xviii.

16. Ibid., *Famine in North Korea*, 55.

17. Ibid., 55.

18. Haggard and Noland ultimately trace the famine back to the "Public Distribution Systems" unequal distribution of food. As they note in the food surveys: "Pyongyang consistently comes out on top, sometimes receiving per person rations that are nearly twice those in less protected provinces." Meanwhile "the most severely affected were urban households in the disadvantaged provinces." Ibid., 68, 70. This breakdown

in the socialist entitlement system is the proximate cause of the famine in their analysis.

19. For a timeline of the North Korean nuclear weapons program see: http://acdis.illinois.edu/resources/arms-control-quick-facts/timeline-of-north-koreas-nuclear-development.html. "For example, in 1999, at the same time that it was cutting commercial grain imports to less than two hundred thousand metric tons, the government allocated scarce foreign exchange to the purchase of forty Mig-21 fighters and eight military helicopters from Kazakhstan." Ibid., 50.

20. Haggard and Noland point out that there was enough food available in North Korea to ensure the survival of the entire population throughout this period. The problem was ultimately one of *distribution*—not an insufficient food supply. Ibid., 46. All of the discussion from 41 to 49 is relevant here.

21. Sen, *Development as Freedom*, 16.

22. Sen, *Identity and Violence: The Illusion of Destiny*, 97.

23. Ibid., 97.

24. Sen, *Development as Freedom*, 145.

25. *The Cambridge History of The Cold War, Volume I, Origins*, 381.

26. Ibid. 381-382.

27. Ibid., 391. Eisenhower also considered the use of nuclear weapons "to assist the French forces under siege in Dienbienphu" in 1954. Holloway notes, however, that Eisenhower made no public nuclear threat in this case.

28. Ibid., 392.

29. Ibid., 387.

30. "Stalin regarded the use of the bomb as an anti-Soviet move, designed to deprive the Soviet Union of strategic gains in the Far East and more generally to give the United States the upper hand in defining the postwar settlement. On August 20, 1945, two weeks to the day after Hiroshima, Stalin signed a decree setting up a Special Committee on the Atomic Bomb, under the chairmanship of Lavrentii P. Beria." Ibid., 377.

# NINE

## Defense

In the previous chapters, the foreign policy of Rawls' ideal democracy was described in greater detail. Rawls rules out the use of force in dealings with peaceful societies. He also outlines policies that can effect change in outlaw regimes—without resorting to violent interventions. Above all, Rawls affirms the duty of assistance.

Interpreted in this manner, *The Law of Peoples* very closely follows the Universal Declaration of Human Rights. But what about the policies of actual existing states since 1948—the year the Universal Declaration was signed? Have the states of the world abandoned the paths of political realism in their speeches and policies? Was there a large change in the behavior of heads of state during this period?

I will not try to answer these questions directly. They are too big for me. What I will do is look at some of the effects of the Cold War on a few newly emergent regimes around the world. And I will conclude with some thoughts on human security in the post-Cold War era.

### 1. THE COLD WAR IN AFRICA

The Cold War—roughly speaking, the conflict between the Soviet Union and the United States of America and its allies—followed World War II. And, unfortunately, this conflict inflicted a significant amount of collateral damage on societies around the globe. The goal of promoting democracy and human rights was obscured by other aims.

The effects of the Cold War on the development of democracy are documented by Sen. In particular, Sen notes that many of the newly emergent, postcolonial regimes of Africa were filled with promise at first, but quickly turned sour:

> Toward the middle of the century the formal ending of empires—British, French, Portuguese, and Belgian—came with a strong promise of democratic development in Africa. Instead, the bulk of the region soon fell prey to authoritarianism and militarism, a breakdown of civil order and educational and health services, and a veritable explosion of local conflicts, intercommunity strife, and civil wars.[1]

And the reason for this is not mysterious. It is a direct result of the conflict between the superpowers during this period:

> The Cold War, which was substantially fought on African soil (though this is rarely acknowledged), made each of the superpowers cultivate military rulers friendly to itself and, perhaps more importantly, hostile to the enemy. When military overlords such as Mobuto Sese Seko of Congo, or Jonas Savimbi of Angola, or whoever, busted social and political orders (and ultimately economic orders too) in Africa, they could rely on support from the Soviet Union or from the United States and its allies, depending on their military alliances.[2]

The situation Sen describes here is exceedingly grim. Providing arms and other forms of assistance to these regimes had disastrous effects on these societies. Heads of state increased in power and were able to pursue their goals with greater force. And there was very little the civilians living in these societies could do to stop these persons.

The lesson here is clear. Superpower rivalry resulted in a pattern of "authoritarianism" and "militarism" that trampled the democratic shoots in many African societies. And this was true despite the fact that the policies of the superpowers were "defensive" in nature. Preventing "the enemy" from gaining an alliance had overwhelmingly negative effects on many African peoples.

*Superpower Aggression*

Sen describes the effects of the Cold War in Africa in the starkest of terms. In Sen's words: "The world powers bear an awesome responsibility for contributing, in the Cold War years, to the subversion of democracy in Africa."[3] And it should be noted that this problem is not limited to various African regimes during this period. Rawls draws attention to the fact that established democracies took measures to overthrow newly emergent democracies around the world. In particular, he notes that: "the United States overturned the democracies of Allende in Chile, Arbenz in Guatemala, Mosaddegh in Iran, and, some would add, the Sandinistas in Nicaragua."[4] And if one asks the question "Why?" Rawls offers this response:

> Whatever the merits of these regimes, covert operations against them were carried out by a government prompted by monopolistic and oligarchic interests without the knowledge of the public. This subterfuge was made easier by the handy appeal to national security in the context of superpower rivalry, which allowed such weak democracies to be cast, however implausibly, as a danger.[5]

The claims in this passage are exact and unsparing. During the Cold War, some emergent democracies could be presented to the public of the established democracies as potential allies of the Soviet Union. And thus they could be cast as dangerous threats—even though the armies and the GDP of these countries at this time were tiny compared to the armies and the GDP of the developed democratic nations.[6] Note also that Rawls does not ascribe these violent interventions to the Cold War per se. Corporate interests were worried about the status of their property, which had been acquired during an earlier colonial period. It is the conflict between colonialism and nationalism—and not the Cold War per se—that lie behind these events. But whatever the rationale here the result was terrible. Fledgling democracies were overthrown in the name of the national interest.[7]

### Effects

Rawls' passage on the suppression of democracies during the Cold War is very damning. The pattern of colonialism in the name of commerce was still at work even though all of these coups were carried out after 1948. And one must recall what the overthrow of a democracy means to Rawls. The ideals of freedom and equality—ideals that are absolutely essential to the protection of *the individual person* within the state—are obscured with other types of language and rhetoric. The possibility of gradual, nonviolent change is also lost.

A second comment: the loss of democracy means the loss of a democracy's political culture and its basic institutions. But once the basic institutions of a society are sabotaged they are not easy to regain. As described earlier, the absence of democracy allows certain heads of state and their families—and other members of the elite of the regime—to control a nation's lawmaking powers and its armed forces indefinitely into the future. What policies could possibly reverse this change *after the fact*?

The options here are not good at all. Perhaps a head of state and other elite will voluntarily abdicate their rule after a period of prolonged nonviolent pressure. But voluntary abdication—or the acceptance of a diminishment of power—depends on a change of heart of the rulers of the regime. And while this has occurred in the last sixty years, no policy can expect every non-democratic head of state to immediately and voluntarily abdicate their power.[8] One must be prepared to take the long view here.

Taking the long view is not easy to do. But after Lenin and Stalin and Khruschev one might find a ruler like Gorbachev. Regimes *can* change as their leaders vary. Another possibility, however, is to encourage the elite within an outlaw regime to fragment into factions. In this way, the power of the outlaw regime is divided against itself.

Intervening in the political relation of another state might appeal to the sensibilities of some political realists. By encouraging factions, the powers of a competitor state might be weakened. But this "policy" basically amounts to the encouragement of civil war in another society. And civil wars are really terrible events. No humane policy can ever promote a civil war.

This point can be made more precise. The political scientists Jack S. Levy and William R. Thompson draw out many features of contemporary civil wars in their joint book *Causes of War*. First, there is the toll on the persons caught up in these wars: "Data from the Correlates of War project show that in the period from 1945 to 1997 there were 23 interstate wars involving 3.3 million battlefield deaths and *108 civil wars involving 11.4 million battlefield deaths.*"[9] (*italics mine*) More persons died in civil wars than in interstate wars during this period.

Second, civil wars tend to be protracted affairs: "On average, civil wars last four times as long as do interstate wars, and approximately three-quarters of the countries experiencing a civil war suffered from at least one additional civil war."[10] There are many reasons why civil wars take a long time to resolve. But a main point is that neither side in many civil wars can quickly win. More precisely: once opposition groups become armed they may not have the power to defeat their regime. But the regime may also lack the power to decisively defeat the opposition group or groups.[11] In this situation, hostilities can persist for a very long time. And if no good faith efforts are made at reconciliation, the civil war can easily resume after a hiatus.

Third, civil wars have devastating effects on the civilian population caught up in these wars. Citing the work of the political scientist Mary Kaldor, Levy and Thompson note that:

> In the early twentieth century, the proportion of civilian war casualties was in the neighborhood of 10-15 percent. *At the end of the same century, civilian war casualties averaged roughly around 80 percent.* Population displacement problems became more severe as well. Conservative estimates of the number of refugees indicated about two and a half million in 1975, ten and a half million in 1985, some eighteen million in 1992, and fourteen and a half million by 1995.[12] (*italics mine*)

The evidence here is unambiguous. Civilians—not combatants—are the disproportionate victims of contemporary war. They die in much larger numbers than the persons fighting the war and can often be forced, because of the fighting itself or because of some other insecurity—for instance, the loss of a dependable income—to leave their homes.

From this point of view, restoring democracy through the promotion of civil war in a state is an extraordinary cruel and violent "policy." Under what circumstances could anyone ever recommend this decision? And how much better would it be to avoid suppressing democracy in the first place?

## 2. LIMITING THE WEAPONS TRADE

The Universal Declaration of Human Rights was ratified by forty-eight nations in 1948—including the United States of America and the Soviet Union. But this did not mean the foreign policy of these states suddenly shifted. And whether this is due to old habits of hostility and suspicion or to specific events—the civil war in China, the Korean War, the policies of Stalin, the dropping of the atomic bombs on civilians in Japan—is a question I cannot answer. But the Cold War had its terrible effects and many of the political problems faced today are rooted in the decisions of this period. To cite just one example: the Soviet invasion of Afghanistan—and the insurgency the United States of America helped to fund and arm to counteract this invasion—helped create the Taliban in Afghanistan.[13] The militancy of Osama bin Laden also began here.[14]

Reflecting on these events is a cause for remorse. Why, exactly, did the Cold War have to break out? Still, the question remains: how can a democracy defend itself given the realities of the post-Cold War era? And what are some of the strategies that can be pursued to advance human rights?

One very clear and immediate step is to avoid repeating the mistakes of the past. Subverting incipient democracies is not a policy that should ever be adopted. Avoiding mistakes is always a good thing. But a second strategy involves putting the powers of collective action to work in a nonviolent way. Coordinated foreign policy can achieve important results.

For instance, according to the Stockholm International Peace Research Institute (SIPRI)—which monitors the global weapons trade—the United Nations has imposed arms embargoes that prohibit giving or trading weapons to several countries and groups. The list of embargoed countries and groups at the time of this writing include: the Taliban (United Nations Security Council Resolution 1390), Al-Qaeda and associated individuals and entities (UNSCR 1390), Cote d'Ivoire (UNSCR 1572), nongovernmental forces in the Democratic Republic of Congo (UNSCR 1493), Eritrea (UNSCR 1907), nongovernmental forces in Iraq (UNSCR 661), Iran (UNSCR 1737), nongovernmental forces in Lebanon (UNSCR 1701), Liberia (UNSCR 788), Libya (UNSCR 1970), North Korea (UNSCR 1718), Somalia (UNSCR 733), and the Darfur region of Sudan (UNSCR 1556).[15]

There are many comments one can make about the strategy of a mandatory embargo. But if one asks the question: "What would be happening right now if these embargoes *were not in place?*" The answer is clear; in the absence of a mandatory embargo, the heads of state involved would find it easier to gain access to conventional weapons. The power of these states and groups would be greater than the powers they currently have.

The arms embargoes currently in force have been established on a "case by case" basis. And, while a draft document of an Arms Trade Treaty has not been produced, such a treaty is currently being negotiated at the United Nations. It stands to reason that a more systematic approach to controlling the global weapons trade could go a long way in advancing human security. Or, to speak more moderately: many problems that currently exist would not be compounded or intensified by more lethal arms.

An Arms Trade Treaty could make a difference to people living everywhere. It is the civilians of a society, one must remember, that are the most likely victims of contemporary war. But what about the potential for trade in regards to *nuclear* weapons? What can collective action accomplish here?

Consider, in this context, the Nuclear Non-Proliferation Treaty. The Nuclear Non-Proliferation Treaty was ratified in 1968 and was meant to freeze the number of nuclear powers in the world. Trading nuclear weapons—and the trade of the components and technology and "know-how" that make possible the building of these weapons—has been banned by all of the countries that have ratified this agreement. In particular, 189 nations have signed this treaty.

Again, there are a number of comments one can make about this strategy. Controlling the trade of nuclear weapons—and the technology and know-how that makes the construction of these weapons possible— is a very complicated objective. The point I would like to lead with, however, is simpler in nature. If one asks the question: "What would have happened if this treaty *were not in place*?" the answer is clear: many more states would have access to nuclear weapons. The destructive powers of any number of regimes would be immeasurably greater than they currently are.

From this point of view, the capacity for collective action—the capacity of many societies to coordinate their foreign policies with each other— has had extraordinarily beneficial effects in the lives of all peoples everywhere. And this is true despite the fact that more can be done.

### 3. PROLIFERATION

Coordinated foreign policy efforts are extremely important for weapons control. If the states that possess nuclear arms thought to themselves: "Let's trade nuclear weapons for revenue" it would be a disaster. But what would happen if a state decided to go it alone and develop nuclear weapons? Is this a viable way to defend one's nation?

In reflecting on this question, it might help to examine an actual case of nuclear proliferation. What happened when a nation decided to "go it alone" in regards to a nuclear defense?

In his essay "India and the Bomb," Sen examines the decision of the Indian government to refrain from signing the Nuclear Non-Proliferation Treaty. More precisely, the Indian government did not sign the Non-Proliferation Treaty in 1968, developed nuclear weapons capability, and conducted a nuclear test first in 1974 (the "Pohkran I" tests) and again in May 1998 (the "Pokhran II" tests). What was the cumulative result of all of these decisions in Sen's analysis?[16]

Well, one might think that India has become more secure. The destructive powers of the Indian state, after all, were increased immeasurably by the development of these weapons. But does this assumption withstand scrutiny? Were the people of India made more secure by the nation's nuclear policy?

Sen's answer to this question is a resounding "No." The people of India are not more secure now than they previously were. The development and testing of nuclear weapons did not increase the individual or collective security of the Indian people. Just the opposite: the people of India are in greater danger now than they were before. There is a higher risk of a terrible violent event in Sen's view since the government of India made this choice.

At first glance, this might seem like a counterintuitive conclusion. Why would increasing one's military power actually decrease one's safety? But if one reflects on the problems inherent in political realism with which this book has been preoccupied, this conclusion should not be surprising. India's decision to develop and test nuclear weapons caused neighboring Pakistan—which also refused to sign the Nuclear Non-Proliferation Treaty in 1968—to follow suit. In Sen's words:

> The five Indian nuclear explosions in Pokhran on 11 and 13 May 1998 were quickly followed by six Pakastani blasts in the Chagai hills the following month. 'The whole mountain turned white' was the Pakistani government's charmed response. The subcontinent was now caught in an overt nuclear confrontation, masquerading as further empowerment of each country.[17]

The possibility of a nuclear exchange between India and Pakistan was laid on top of preexisting hostilities. There was now a *new* threat, one that did not previously exist before. But shouldn't India and Pakistan have been less likely to engage *in conventional attacks* against each other now that each state possessed "the bomb"? Didn't "mutually assured destruction" or some variant doctrine lead to greater caution in the use of conventional military force? Sen's response to this question is also a resounding "No." Sen states that:

> . . . there is nothing to indicate that the likelihood of conventional war is, in fact, reduced by the nuclearization of India and Pakistan. Indeed, hot on the heels of the nuclear blasts, the two countries did undergo a major military confrontation in the Kargil district of Kashmir. The Kargil conflict, which occurred within a year of the nuclear blasts of India and Pakistan, was in fact the first military conflict between the two in nearly thirty years.[18]

This again might seem counterintuitive. Why would India and Pakistan become *more* likely to engage in conventional hostilities, given that both nations have joined the "nuclear club"?

The key point here is a shift in the balance of power that followed nuclear proliferation. Sen indicates that India has always maintained a stronger conventional army than Pakistan: "India had—and has—massive superiority over Pakistan in conventional military strength."[19] But after India encouraged Pakistan to choose the path of nuclear proliferation—by first refusing to sign the NPT, and then later through the Pokhran I and especially the Pokhran II tests—India could not use this conventional superiority for fear of a Pakistani nuclear reprisal. The ability of India to respond to the Kargil border conflict was actually *constrained* by India's decision to develop and test new nuclear weapons.[20]

## Luck

Sen's analysis of India's decision to proliferate is critical in the extreme. Far from making the Indian people more secure, it increased the exposure of the Indian people to conventional and nuclear attacks. As Sen notes, one must "[take] into account the responses from others that would be generated by one's pursuit of military strength."[21] Escalating *actions* almost inevitably lead to escalating *"counteractions,"* Sen says.

The key insight of Sen's analysis of nuclear proliferation lies here. Actions cannot be understood in a vacuum. Agents *respond to* the actions of others. Increasing the strength of one's own military will lead others to increase the strength of their forces. Nor can heads of state say: "we want the power of nuclear weapons but will never use them." As Sen points out, the development of a weapon is meaningful only if one is willing to use that weapon:

> Implicitly or explicitly, an eventuality of actual use has to be among the possible scenarios that must be contemplated, if some benefit is to be obtained from the possession and deployment of nuclear weapons. To hold the belief that nuclear weapons are useful but must never be used lacks cogency . . .

The conclusion Sen draws from this insight is startling. It was not so much that the strategy of nuclear deterrence was successful during the Cold War or in the post-Cold War era. Instead, the absence of a nuclear "exchange" might be attributable to other factors: "I think we have to recognize that the peace of nuclear confrontation in the Cold War partly resulted *from luck*, and was not preordained." [22] (*italics mine*) In particular, it has resulted from the accidental fact that—and here Sen quotes Churchill—"no dictators in the mood of Hitler when he found himself in his final dugout" have controlled nuclear weapons. [23]

### Nuclear Deterrence

"Increasing the power of the state is key to security." "It is better to be the militarily stronger state than the military weaker state in a confrontation." "It is best to develop and maintain an arsenal of nuclear weapons." These claims might seem like common sense. But they are also part of the problem. Becoming a member of the "nuclear club" in fact makes a country less safe than before.

It is from this point of view that one can begin to understand Sen's recommendations for national defense. In particular, Sen calls for treaties that abolish nuclear weapons altogether and sharply constrain the conventional weapons trade. He states, ". . . the world order on weapons needs a change and in particular requires an effective and rapid *disarmament*, particularly in nuclear arsenals." [24] (*italics mine*)

Without a coordinated effort towards the reduction and eventual elimination of nuclear weapons, the situation is unstable and can tend toward truly unthinkable events. The best defense is *collective action*—not the newest weapon system.

Sen's argument about nuclear and conventional weapon reduction amounts to a gigantic reversal of current practice. But this does not mean

Sen is wrong. What is stable, one must ask, about a planet where many heads of state possess incredibly lethal arms? How exactly does an indefinite escalation of military power get the world to a stable peace? But what about Rawls' perspective on these questions? More precisely: how does Rawls think about a democracy's military strength?

On the question of nuclear weapons, Rawls emphasizes a different problem than the one emphasized by Sen. Rawls assumes expansionist states that deny human rights will continue to exist. As a consequence, Rawls believes "some nuclear weapons need to be retained"—to deter these states from violent expansion. Liberal democracies, Rawls continues must also "make sure [outlaw] regimes do not obtain and use [nuclear] weapons against liberal or decent peoples."[25] In this way, no decent society will ever face the problem the Melians faced.

The sentence on nuclear deterrence in *The Law of Peoples* is very important. It calls attention—in my opinion—to a strand of defensive political realism in Rawls' foreign policy. Rawls does not totally break free from this theory.

Or, to put this point another way: Rawls affirms the foreign policy of reciprocity and assistance. Democracies must promote human rights through its actions and policies and refrain from enhancing the powers of outlaw regimes. And there is no doubt that Rawls supports a coordinated effort to reduce the number of nuclear weapons in the world and prevent nuclear proliferation. But when it comes to dealing with truly expansionist outlaw regimes—which can sometimes be "among the more effectively organized and economically advanced societies" of their time—Rawls believes a democracy must maintain a nuclear arsenal to restrain these states.[26]

Interpreted in this manner, Rawls would support non-proliferation and a nuclear arsenal reduction. But he would not call for the total abolition of all nuclear weapons. Allowing too great a military asymmetry to develop between outlaw regimes and democratic or decent societies is a mistake.

## 4. POLITICAL CULTURE AND THE USE OF FORCE

Rawls and Sen diverge on the question of nuclear deterrence. Sen is entirely skeptical about this doctrine. In Sen's view, the possession of nuclear weapons leads to proliferation, conflict spirals and the greater likelihood of a terrible outcome. In Rawls's view, on the other hand, possessing nuclear weapons can serve as a deterrent against outlaw regimes—both those that exist now and those that will exist in the future. Above all, Rawls does not believe the democracies of the world will always be the most powerful states in terms of conventional military power. Decent societies cannot fall into the military weaker position—relative to the outlaw regimes of their time.

Rawls and Sen differ on the question of nuclear defense. But why is Rawls less concerned about the possibility of a conflict spiral in the context of a liberal democracy's possession of nuclear weapons? What justifies Rawls' stance here?

This question can be asked another way. Early on in *The Law of Peoples* Rawls argued that, "One strong state possessed of military and economic power and embarked on expansion and glory is sufficient to perpetuate the cycle of war and preparation for war."[27]

Here Rawls is very clear about the possibility of a conflict spiral. An arms race and a pattern of escalating hostility is the predictable result of *political realism*. But couldn't one make the same point about nuclear weapons? Why doesn't a democracy's decision to possess nuclear weapons touch off several rounds of nuclear proliferation? From an historical point of view, the decision of the United States to develop—*and use*—a nuclear weapon was interpreted as a threat by the Soviet Union.[28] The Soviet Union, in turn, decided to respond by developing its own nuclear weapon. And this led to an extraordinarily dangerous crisis spiral. During the Cuban Missile Crisis—as has been acknowledged by both sides—*the existence of humanity* on earth was at risk. Similarly, the decision of India to pursue nuclear weapons played a role in the decision of Pakistan to develop and test nuclear weapons. This, again, resulted in very grave danger for the peoples involved. In Sen's estimation, "Bangladesh is probably now the safest country to live in, in the subcontinent."[29]

In both of these cases, the decision *of a democracy* to develop nuclear weapons helped intensify a conflict spiral. Why couldn't these types of events—which have happened before—happen again?

Rawls does not address this question directly. However, Rawls does believe that the political culture of a society ultimately determines how that society uses its military power.[30] *The beliefs* citizens and leaders have about the use of military force matter in Rawls' account. But Rawls' discussion of political culture also applies to his discussion of nuclear deterrence. As long as the political culture of the ideal democracy affirms human rights its possession of nuclear weapons is not threatening to other nations.

In this interpretation, the ideal democracy's possession of nuclear weapons is for defensive purposes only. A "preemptive strike" scenario involving nuclear weapons is never a possibility in Rawls' account. And because the possession of these weapons is for defensive purposes only — *and this fact is understood by other nations* — an escalating response is not triggered. The *trust* the ideal democracy has gained with the rest of the world is the decisive factor here.

## CONCLUDING THOUGHTS

I understand Rawls' reliance on the political culture of the ideal democracy. But I do not find it persuasive. Rawls is appealing to a political culture that does not yet exist to justify a policy towards nuclear weapons which most definitely do exist and which can cause immeasurable harm. This, in my view, is not a good idea. Beliefs about the use of force can vary greatly within any society. The political parties in a democracy, for instance, can affirm different principles regarding both the role of the military in policy *and* the use of weapons. But this point does not even need to be framed in terms of partisan differences. Individuals are fallible and make mistakes under pressure. Indeed, individuals make errors even without pressure. No political culture, however ideal, can fully guard against human fallibility.

In this case, appealing to ideal theory to guide nonideal theory can lead one astray. And if there is anything that deserves criticism in *The Law of Peoples* it is Rawls' treatment of the "Supreme Emergency Exemption" in conjunction with his comments about nuclear deterrence. A policy of nuclear deterrence is founded on the willingness to actually kill millions of *civilians* in another country. I cannot imagine any justification for this possibility.[31] And the argument Rawls' makes on these matters — e.g., the statesmen will know when it is necessary to target civilians (i.e., in cases of supreme emergency only) and when it is impermissible to do so (in all other cases) — is hard to interpret and can be easily distorted during a crisis.[32]

Rawls discussion of deterrence and the supreme emergency exemption is not persuasive. But the comment I would like to end with, however, does not involve the Supreme Emergency Exemption—with which I do not agree. I would like to finish with a point about the use of a society's finite resources. Sen notes that India's commitment to developing and maintaining a nuclear arsenal had an overwhelmingly negative affect on human security in India and Pakistan. The possession of nuclear weapons did not leave the people living in these societies more safe. Sen, however, also notes that nuclear weapons carry with them a very substantial opportunity-cost for the societies that choose to maintain them:

> Recently, C. Rammanohar Reddy, a distinguished commentator, has estimated that the cost of nuclearization is something around half of one per cent of the gross domestic product per year. This might not sound like much, but it is large enough *if we consider the alternative uses of these resources.* For example, it has been estimated that the additional costs of providing elementary education for every child with neighborhood schools at every location in the country would cost roughly the same amount of money. The proportion of illiteracy in the Indian population is still about 40 percent, and it is about 55 percent in Pakistan.[33]
> (*italics mine*)

Public education for every Indian child could be achieved if the amount of money spent on India's nuclear weapons program was instead spent on developing a system of "neighborhood schools." And one should recall, in this context, Sen's comments about the importance of literacy in general, and female literacy in particular. By expending resources on a nuclear weapons program that makes Indians less secure, literacy levels in India are lower than they could be, Indian society is severely divided between the children who receive a formal education and the children who do not, there is more childhood mortality, and the population of the country is continuing to grow at an unsustainable level.[34] This is a gigantic loss to accept in exchange for no gain. Nor is Sen's criticism here aimed at India alone. The mistake that is harming the civilians of India is also harming the civilians of Pakistan. The foreign policy of these nations is capturing the domestic policy of these nations—to terrible effect.

The argument Sen makes in the chapter "India and the Bomb" is critical in the extreme. Why, exactly, is the possession of nuclear weapons a good idea? What benefit do these weapons bring to the nations that build them? This argument, however, can also be generalized, albeit in a cautious way. According to the Stockholm International Peace Research Institute, cumulative military spending—very roughly, the amount of money spent by each nation on its armed forces added together—has hovered around 2.5% of global GDP for the past 10 years. [35] This is a gargantuan amount of money and amounts to over a trillion and a half dollars per year when it is all said and done. Is this military spending making the earth a more secure place for humanity? And if more than fifteen trillion dollars of military spending a decade is not making humanity better off—and it most assuredly is not—why not find new uses for some of these resources? There is any number of pressing problems that remain unaddressed. Would it not, for instance, be better to create a "neighborhood school" for all children everywhere than to continue to research and produce newer and better versions of the weapons almost everyone fervently hopes will never be used? It is hard to imagine how the maintenance and expansion of the conventional and nuclear arsenals of the world is really the best thing.

From this point of view, a reduction in global military spending through an Arms Trade Treaty and other measures—coupled with the redirection of this spending to the creation of schools—could accomplish an incredible amount of good for all people. It is the kind of adjustment to foreign policy that would genuinely benefit humanity *as a whole* without, one might add, raising a single penny through an additional tax. And if it is too much to expect all of the nations of the world to simultaneously check or curb their military trades and expenditures—although this step would clearly be an incredibly beneficial step, reducing the possibility of conflict spirals, and marking a kind of collective action that would be truly amazing to behold—"multilateral" and "bilateral" decisions can still be taken.

For instance, the United States of America and Russia are currently discussing further reductions of their nuclear arsenals. [36] This is a very positive development. With every reduction in nuclear arsenals the world is a bit safer. Moreover, the resources freed up by this coordinated disarmament can be put to far more desirable uses then "assured destruction." If the two superpowers caused such great harm to the emergent nations of the world during the Cold War period, perhaps some effort could be made at restitution through a development fund. Acknowledging past harms—and making some effort to redress these harms—is always just.

Finally, it should be pointed out that certain steps do not require agreements between countries. The elected leaders of a single democracy can always adjust its foreign policy on its own. The United States of America—which spends more on its armed forces than the next fourteen nations *combined* and which still possesses an exceedingly large nuclear arsenal, even after the START and NEW START treaties—could, for instance, decide to rebalance its foreign policy priorities.[37] A great deal can be achieved in the world through the duty of assistance.

## NOTES

1. Sen, *Identity and Violence: The Illusion of Destiny,* 95-96.

2. Ibid, 96-97.

3. Ibid, 98.

4. Rawls, *The Law of Peoples,* 53.

5. Ibid., 58.

6. The claim that the Melians could aid the Spartans, the enemies of Athens, justified the invasion of Melos in Athenian eyes—even though Melos was a very small city-state compared to Athens at this time. See Thucydides, *The Pelopponesian War,* 352.

7. Rawls appears to be referencing the British Anglo-Iranian Oil Company in Iran, the United Fruit Company in Guatemala, and the Purina Company in Chile—among other western corporate interests—in this passage.

8. The King of Nepal voluntarily ceded his control of the armed forces of Nepal in 2006. This action played a crucial role in diminishing a ten-year period of civil conflict in this country.

9. Jack S. Levy and William R. Thompson, *Causes of War,* 185.

10. Ibid., 186.

11. The civil war in Nepal followed this pattern. At the time of this writing, Nepal still lacks an agreed upon constitution.

12. Ibid., 191. See also Mary Kaldor *New and Old Wars: Organized Violence in a Global Era,* p. 100-101.

13. "The Soviet Union poured some $5 billion a year into Afghanistan to subdue the Mujaheddin or a total of $45 billion . . . The United States committed some four to five billion dollars between 1980 and 1992 in aid to the Mujaheddin. U.S. funds were matched by Saudi Arabia and together with support from other European and Islamic countries, the Mujaheddin received a total of over US$10 billion. Most of this aid was in the form of lethal modern weaponry given to a simple agricultural people who used it with devastating results." Ahmed Rashid, *Taliban: Militant Islam, Oil, and Fundamentalism in Central Asia,* 18.

14. Ibid., 131-142.

15. The Stockholm Institute of Peace Research Initiatives maintains a database of countries embargoed through acts of the security council of the United Nations. This list is updated as new resolutions are passed. http://www.sipri.org/databases/embargoes

16. Sen discusses the role China played in the decision of India to pursue a nuclear weapon, but his basic contention—that India should not have pursued a strategy of nuclear deterrence—is not altered by this assessment. See Sen, *The Argumentative Indian,* 265-266.

17. Sen, *The Argumentative Indian*, 256.

18. Ibid., 260.

19. Ibid., 263. In this passage, Sen seems to affirm the need for a conventional army that is stronger than—or comparable to—its adversary.

20. Ibid., 261.

21. Ibid., 252. Sen is describing the foreign policy views of Rabindrinath Tagore—articulated in 1917—in this passage.

22. Ibid., 262.

23. Ibid., 261.

24. Ibid., 267.

25. John Rawls, *The Law of Peoples*, 9.

26. Ibid., 48.

27. Ibid., 48.

28. The United States of America decided to develop nuclear weapons in response to the potential threat of the German nuclear program: "The American effort to build an atomic bomb was the direct result of the fear that Germany had the intent and ability to do the same. In fact, by the fall of 1939 the Germans had begun investigating the possibility of building a bomb. The effort was led by physicist Werner Heisenberg, winner of the Nobel Prize in 1926 for his work on quantum theory and nuclear physics." Michael Kort, *The Columbia Guide to Hiroshima and The Bomb*, 25.

29. Sen, *The Argumentative Indian*, 258.

30. Rawls, *The Law of Peoples*, 102-103.

31. Sen quotes Arundhati Roy to draw out the point that imagining the outcomes of a nuclear exchange is not really possible: "Our cities and forests, our fields and villages will burn for days. Rivers will turn to poison. The air will become fire. The wind will spread the flames. When everything there is to burn has burned and the fire dies, smoke will rise and shut out the sun." How Sen asks can this "eventuality" ever be part of a "wise policy of national self defense"? Sen, *The Argumentative Indian*, 257.

32. As Michael Walzer observes, during the Cold War the notion of a "supreme emergency" was not understood episodically. Instead, *all* moments were "supreme emergencies": "Supreme emergency has become a permanent condition. Deterrence is a way of coping with that condition, and though it is a bad way, there may well be no other that is practical in a world of sovereign and suspicious states." Walzer, *Just and Unjust Wars: A Moral Argument with Historical Illustrations*, 274. But, as Walzer notes, what meaning does the term "supreme emergency" possess if all moments are "supreme emergencies"? Notice also Walzer's use of the language of defensive political realism in this passage. A condition of unending hostility seems fated here—although Walzer softens this claim somewhat at the end of this chapter (p. 282-283).

33. Sen, *The Argumentative Indian*, 259-260.

34. See chapter 3 above.

35. The Stockholm Institute of Peace Research Initiatives maintains a database on military expenditures that is updated as new information is released into the public domain. See the table on world military expenditures in the SIPRI 2013 yearbook for more precise information on global military spending since the end of the Cold War. http://www.sipri.org/yearbook/2013/03

36. Gorbachev and Reagan agreed to the "START" treaty (the Strategic Arms Reduction Treaty) at the Reykjavik summit of 1986. In 2010, the United States of America and Russia signed the "NEW START" treaty.

37. According to the SIPRI Trends in World Military Expenditure, 2012 the United States of America's military spending in 2012 was 688 billion dollars. This amount is substantially larger than the military spending of China (166 billion dollars), Russia (90.7 billion dollars), the United Kingdom (60.8 billion dollars), Japan (59.3 billion dollars), France (58.9 billion dollars), Saudi Arabia (56.7 billion dollars), India (46.1 billion dollars), Germany (45.8 billion dollars), Italy (34.0 billion dollars), Brazil (33.1 billion dollars), South Korea (31.7 billion dollars), Australia (26.2 billion dollars), Canada (22.5 billion dollars) and Turkey (18.2 billion dollars). http://books.sipri.org/product_info?c_product_id=458. According to the Department of State website, as of September 1st, 2012 the United States possessed 1722 "Strategic Offensive Arms" including "warheads on deployed ICBMs, on Deployed SLBMs, and Nuclear Warheads Counted for Deployed Heavy Bombers." The Russian Federation possessed 1499 "Strategic Offensive Arms" including "warheads on deployed ICBMs, on SLBMs, and Nuclear Warheads Counted for Deployed Heavy Bombers." http://www.state.gov/t/avc/rls/201216.htm

# Bibliography

Aamodt, Sandra and Sam Wang. *Welcome to Your Child's Brain*. New York: Bloomsbury USA, 2011.

Appiah, Kwame Anthony. *Cosmopolitanism: Ethics in a World of Strangers*. New York: Norton, 2006.

Arneil, Barbara. *John Locke and America: The Defence of English Colonialism*. Oxford Clarendon Press, 1996.

Chappell, Vere, ed. *The Cambridge Companion to Locke*. Cambridge: Cambridge University Press, 1994.

Dreze, Jean and Amartya Sen. *Hunger and Public Action*. Oxford: Oxford Clarendon Press, 1989.

Eichengreen, Barry. *Golden Fetters: The Gold Standard and The Great Depression, 1919-1939*. Oxford: Oxford University Press, 1995.

Glendon, Mary Ann. *A World Made New: Eleanor Roosevelt and The Universal Declaration of Human Rights*. New York: Random House Trade Paperback Edition, 2002.

Haggard, Stephen, and Marcus Noland. *Famine in North Korea: Markets, Aid, Reform*. New York: Columbia University Press, 2007.

Kaldor, Mary. *New and Old Wars: Organized Violence in a Global Era*. Stanford, CA: Stanford University Press, 1999.

Kant, Immanuel. *Groundwork for the Metaphysics of Morals*. Indianapolis: Hackett, 1993.

Kort, Michael. *The Columbia Guide to Hiroshima and The Bomb*. New York: Columbia University Press, 2007.

Leffler, Melvyn P., and Odd Arne Westad, eds. *Cambridge History of The Cold War Vol. 1*. Cambridge: Cambridge University Press, 2010.

Levy, Jack S. and Thompson, William R. *Causes of War*. Chichester, West Sussex: Wiley-Blackwell, 2010.

Lichtblau, Eric. *The Holocaust Just Got More Shocking*. March 03, 2013. http://www.nytimes.com/2013/03/03/sunday-review/the-holocaust-just-got-more-shocking.html?pagewanted=all&_r=2&.

Locke, John. *A Letter Concerning Toleration*. Edited by James H. Tully. Translated by William Popple. Indianapolis, Iniana: Hackett Publishing Company, 1983.

———. *Two Treatises of Government*. Student Edition. Edited by Peter Laslett. Cambridge: Cambridge University Press, 1988.

Machiavelli, Niccolo. *The Prince*. Second Edition. Translated by Harvey C. Mansfield. Chicago: University of Chicago Press, 1985.

Martin, Rex, and David A. Reidy, eds. *Rawls's Law of Peoples: A Realistic Utopia?* Malden, MA: Blackwell, 2006.

Mill, John Stuart. *Utilitarianism*. Indianapolis: Hackett, 2001.

Morens, Jeffrey K., and David M. Taubenberger. 1918 Influenza Outbreak: The Mother of All Pandemics. January 2006. www.ncbi.nlm.nih.gov/pmc/articles/PMC3291398/ (accessed December 26, 2012).

Nathanson, Stephen. *Terrorism and the Ethics of War*. Cambridge: Cambridge University Press, 2010.

Nussbaum, Martha C. *Women and Human Development: The Capabilities Approach*. Cambridge: Cambridge University Press, 2000.

Pogge, Thomas. *John Rawls: His Life and Theory of Justice*. Oxford: Oxford University Press, 2007.

———. *World Poverty and Human Rights*. Cambridge: Polity Press, 2002.

Rashid, Ahmed. *Taliban: Militant Islam, Oil and Fundamentalism in Central Asia*. 2nd edition. New Haven: Yale University Press, 2010.

Rawls, John. *A Theory of Justice*. Revised Edition. Cambridge: The Belknap Press of Harvard University, 1999.

———. *Justice as Fairness: A Restatement*. Edited by Erin Kelly. Cambridge: The Belknap Press of Harvard University, 2001.

———. *Political Liberalism*. Cambridge: The Belknap Press of Harvard University, 1993.

———. *The Law of Peoples with "The Idea of Public Reason Revisited"*. Cambridge, MA: Harvard University Press, 1999.

Sen, Amartya. *Development as Freedom*. New York: Anchor Books, 1999.

———. *Identity and Violence: The Illusion of Destiny*. New York: Norton , 2006.

———. *Poverty and Famines: An Essay on Entitlement and Deprivation*. Oxford: Oxford University Press, 1981.

———. *The Argumentative Indian*. New York: Picador, 2005.

———. *The Idea of Justice*. Cambridge, MA: The Belknap Press of Harvard University, 2009.

Stein, Walter, ed. *Nuclear Weapons and Christian Conscience*. London: The Merlin Press, 1965.

Stockholm Institute of Peace Research Initiatives. *2013 SIPRI Yearbook*. http://www.sipri.org/yearbook/2013/03 .

———. *Arms Embargoes Database*. www.sipri.org/databases/embargoes.

———. *Trends in World Military Expenditure, 2012*. April 15, 2013. http://books.sipri.org/product_info?c_product_id=458.

The Journal of the American Medical Association. http://jama.jamanetwork.com/article.aspx?articleid=185509 (accessed December 26, 2012).

The National Archives (United Kingdom). *The Great Plague of 1665-6*. www.nationalarchives.gov.uk/education/lesson49.htm (accessed December 26, 2012).

The Program for Arms Control, Disarmament and International Security. *Timeline of North Korea's Nuclear Development*. 2013. http://acdis.illinois.edu/resources/arms-control-quick-facts/timeline-of-north-koreas-nuclear-development.html.

The World Bank. *World Development Report 2012: Gender Equality and Development*. Washington DC: The World Bank, 2011.

Thucydides. *The Landmark Thucydides: A Comprehensive Guide to The Pelopponesian War*. Edited by Robert B. Strassler. Translated by Richard Crawley. New York: Free Press, 1996.

United Nations Development Programme. *Human Development Report 2011*. www.unhdr.org/content/undp/en/home/librarypage/hdr/human-developmentreport2011.html (accessed December 26, 2012).

United Nations Population Fund. www.unfpa.org/public.

United States of America Department of State. *New START Treaty Aggregate Numbers of Strategic Offensive Arms.* November 30, 2012. http://www.state.gov/t/avc/rls/201216.htm.

Universal Declaration of Human Rights. 1948.

Walzer, Michael. *Just and Unjust Wars: A Moral Argument with Historical Illustrations.* New York: Basic Books, 2006.

World Health Organization. *World Malaria Report 2011 Fact Sheet* . www.who.int/world_malaria_report_2011_factsheet.pdf.

# Author Bio

Neal Leavitt is a lecturer in the humanities at Boston University. He received his doctorate in philosophy from Boston College and his bachelor of arts in philosophy from Harvard University. He lives with his wife Irene in Cambridge and hopes one day to hike the length of the Himalayas.

# Index